Student Guide for Internal Assessment in Biology

This Guide is aimed at helping you with the asse t –

- **Design**
- **Data Collection and Processing**
- **Conclusion and Evaluation**

- but it can also be used for a practical based Extended Essay.

There is also an extensive section on statistical analysis. Although this is not strictly required for IA it is often easy to do and adds very considerably to your Data Processing and Conclusion.

Each section starts with a table that quotes directly from the Internal Assessment Criteria and Aspects, but only for a 'Complete' level since this is what we are focused on. Then follows a list of the headings under which you should write your report. Using these headings has three functions –

- It makes the overall appearance of your report look good;
- It reduces the likelihood of you missing out important criteria;
- It makes the marking much easier and hence more likely that your assessor will give you a good mark.

I would strongly recommend that you do your practical reports with a word processor such as Microsoft Word. You can then set up a template file with all the subheadings and you then simply delete the headings you don't need. I have put a template on page 61 which you can copy. Also it allows you to make changes easily – this very often happens when you are planning the Method or doing the Evaluations. Also you can embed Excel spreadsheets and use these to do all the calculations and to draw the graphs when you come to the Data Processing section. In Section 1.5 on page 57 I have shown some useful shortcuts for typing cm^3, ^0C and ± instantly without having to repeatedly format.

The font I have used is Arial 10 which gives a clean appearance to the text.

This Guide uses the 2007 / 2010 versions of Microsoft Word and Excel. There is an Appendix which shows how Word/Excel 2003 can be used to insert error bars on graphs.

I would like to thank my departmental colleagues Tony Stuart and Chris Tavare for their valuable help and advice, Chris Hall, (an IB IA Moderator), Dr Gillian Williams, and also my students for their suggestions.
As with all of my OSC Guides any comments from you would be appreciated so that I can make improvements to help other students.

Ashby Merson-Davies

Contents

Section 1.1

Design

Design	Defining the problem and selecting variables	Controlling variables	Developing a method for collection of data
Complete	Formulates a focused problem / research question and identifies the relevant variables.	Designs a method for the effective control of the variables.	Develops a method that allows for the collection of sufficient relevant data.

Design should have six sub-headings.

- **Research Question**
- **Background Information**
- **Variables**
- **Apparatus**
- **Risk Assessment**
- **Method**

Research Question

This has to be precise so that it is clear what you intend to do. The simplest and easiest way is –

What is the effect of X on Y?

For example *'What is the effect of temperature on the rate of movement of chloroplasts in Elodea?'* Then your independent variable is X (temperature) and your dependent variable is Y (rate of movement). Here is a poor example – *How does light affect the behaviour of woodlice?* Why is this poor? We do not know what aspect of light is being used – colour perhaps? Maybe intensity? And what woodlouse behaviour? Rate of turning? Speed? So let's re-write it correctly. *What is the effect of changing light intensity on the speed at which woodlice move?* Your independent variable is light intensity and the dependent variable is speed.

Here is a slightly different type – '*How do differences in light intensity affect the thickness of beech leaves?'*

Background Information

Include information relating only to your Research Question. It would be informative and valuable to put forward a hypothesis (see page 40) with your biological reasoning behind it. You can then refer to this in the Conclusion and Evaluation section.

Variables

Investigations fall into two categories, experiments or correlations.

An experiment is where you are looking at the effect on something of you changing something else. It is therefore designed around variables that you have controlled or manipulated in some way.

Variables fall into four categories –

- Dependent;
- Independent;
- Controlled;
- Uncontrolled.

A correlation is where you have collected sets of data that you want to compare. It is also designed around variables though this time the variables for both X and Y axes are measured.

Look at the three research questions above. The first and second are experiments and the third a correlation. I'll say more about correlations when dealing with scattergraphs on page 30.

Which type of investigation you have determines the type of analysis that you can carry out. This is shown on the statistics route planner on page 39.

The Dependent Variable

- This is what are you going to measure and it should be specified clearly. So '*Rate of reaction*' is not good enough, but '*Volume of oxygen gas released*' is precise and measurable. (Note the use of the word 'volume' – **do not** use 'amount').
- This will be the Y-axis of your graph.
- Time sometimes causes a problem. It is possible to design an investigation with time as the independent variable. However you should not. Always have time as the dependent variable or as a controlled variable.

The Independent Variable

- This is the one that you manipulate to have a *range* of values.
- It will be the X-axis of your graph.
- Choosing the range - important points to keep in mind.
  - It must be selected so that it will allow you to analyse your results and draw a conclusion.
  - There should be a minimum of 6 values. Since you should do repeats as well this is probably the most you will be able to do in the time limits normally imposed. In an extended investigation such as for an Extended Essay you should do more.
  - What values in the range? Initially perhaps an even spread of values, but if you have a change of direction such as with enzymes, then do 2 or 3 more values around this region if you can.
- Controls. Some experiments will benefit from the use of one or more controls. For example if you are investigating the effect of pH on enzyme activity then controls would be substrate with acid or alkali and no enzyme. This would show if the pH alone affects the substrate. Other examples would be the effect of coloured light on the behaviour of woodlice where the control would be white light, or a hydrogen peroxide and catalase concentration investigation where the control would be 0% catalase, ie. distilled water.

The Controlled Variables

- There are a number of other variables that will affect the investigation, and so as many of these as possible must be kept constant. Examples could be –

  - Total volume of a reaction mixture.
  - Temperature.
  - pH.
  - Concentration of solutions.
  - Surface area.
  - Time.
  - Light intensity.
  - Source of biological material used.

The Uncontrolled Variables

- There may be some factors that you simply cannot eliminate or control completely, such as some environmental conditions or certain features of living organisms, but you should try to minimise the effect they will have.
- Think carefully about these though as with care they could often be controlled, eg. room temperature – could you use a water bath? Light through the lab windows – could you close the blinds or shade the apparatus?
- If you really cannot control them then you should **monitor** them if possible so that repeats can be done if there are large changes that could affect the quality of your data.
- Monitored data must be recorded along with the raw data so you can refer to in your Evaluation.

Tabulating Variables

A very simple and effective way to present the variables in your report is in a table as shown below.

Dependent Variable	• This is the one you will measure.
Independent Variable	• This is the one you manipulate over a range of values. • Include the range of values you are going to use.
Controlled Variables	• These are all the ones that you control at a fixed value. • Put these in a list.
Uncontrolled Variables	• These are the ones you have no control over. • Put these in a list.

When you come to the end of your investigation you may want to extend it further by changing variables around. Thus the independent variable can become a controlled variable, and one of the controlled variables can become the independent variable.

For example, suppose you were investigating the effect of temperature on enzyme activity, then pH of the reaction mixture must be a controlled variable. You could then investigate the effect of changing pH at a controlled temperature.

Referencing Sources

These must be written alphabetically in the correct format, and this varies depending on the source you are using.

Books

Douglas, A.E. *Symbiotic Interactions.* Oxford University Press. 1994
Merson-Davies, A. IB Biology: *Genetics Made Easy Standard Level.* Oxford Study Courses. 2012
Roberts, M. Reiss, M. Monger, G. *Advanced Biology*, Nelson. 2000
Walpole, B. Merson-Davies, A. Dann, L. *Biology for the IB Diploma.* Cambridge University Press. 2011

Journals

Knight, J. *Metal heads.* New Scientist. 26 August 2000
Read, A. 'Gene therapy', *Biological Sciences Review*, Vol. 6, No.1, pp22-24.

Internet

Britannica.com. *The Kikuyu: an East African People.* 3 March 1996.
www.brit.com/eastafrica/kenya/kikuyu.htm. 1 September 2000

SI Units

You must use Standard International (SI) units.

Measurement	SI Units and accepted non SI units	Symbols
Distance	metres, centimetres, millimetres	m, cm, mm
Mass	kilograms, grams	kg, g
Volume	decimetres cubed, centimetres cubed	dm^3, cm^3
Concentration	moles, millimoles	mol, mmol
Time	seconds, minutes	s, min

In column headings of tables when the unit is 'per', as in centimetres per minute, always use the minus sign, as in cm min^{-1}. Never use / as this is used to separate the description from the units.
Example – Rate of movement of bubble / cm min^{-1}. Note the single space between cm and min and a single space either side of the /.
In text, such as when writing the Method you should use per eg centimetres per minute – see page 7.

Samples, Sampling and Replicates

When collecting data for an experiment you should aim to do repeats so that you have at least two consistent readings. This may mean doing more than just one repeat. See p16 for more information.

Don't forget that you may be able to add **raw** data collected by other students to your own to increase sample size or as replicates. However you **must** indicate which your data is and which belongs to other students. You should **not** collect processed data as the processing must be done by you.

If you have enough data you will be able to do further statistical analysis, such as calculate standard deviation (see pages 18 – 19) or standard error (see page 58), which is much better..

When collecting data for a correlation we will be collecting a sample, but again we should aim to obtain as large a sample as possible. Between 7 and 30 is usually sufficient to make any analysis meaningful - see the Statistics section pages 38 – 56 and also pages 58/9. Furthermore, where relevant, a sample should be random. For example if you suspected that there might be a correlation between the surface area of leaves on a bush and the height above ground, then it would not be sensible to pick samples from one branch on one side. Once again you may be able to use the data collected by other students.

Abbreviations, Chemical Symbols, and Capital Letters

- Never use abbreviations and chemical symbols in text such as in the Method.
  eg. I measured out 10cm^3 of H_2O into the beaker – wrong.
  I measured out 10cm^3 of water into the beaker – right.
  I measured the movement of the bubble in cm per min – wrong.
  I measured the movement of the bubble in centimetres per minute – right.
- The words for chemical substances do not have capital letters.
  eg. I measured out 10cm^3 each of Water and Hydrogen Peroxide into labelled beakers – wrong.
  I measured out 10cm^3 each of water and hydrogen peroxide into labelled beakers – right.

Apparatus

- It is helpful to write a list of all the equipment and materials you are going to use.
- You must use SI units – see page 6.
- Select equipment that will allow you to be precise, eg. do not use a 250cm^3 measuring cylinder to measure out 10cm^3 – use a 10cm^3 measuring cylinder or 10cm^3 syringe.
- You must be precise about the materials such as volume and concentration, eg. '500cm^3 1mol dm^{-3} glucose solution' and not 'glucose solution' or worse still 'glucose'.
- A fully detailed and labelled drawing of how the apparatus will be set up can also be helpful. Remember though that if the set-up is simple a drawing is not necessary and will take up a lot of time. Never draw pictures of stopwatches, test tube racks, stands, Bunsen burners, matches etc. List these as 'Additional Apparatus'.

See page 57 for a tip on how to type cm^3 quickly in Word.

Risk Assessment

It is essential that you work safely, both for yourself and other students around you in the laboratory.

- Will you be using any sharp items such as dissecting instruments or a knife for cutting?
- Will you be using a Bunsen burner or very hot water?
- Will you be using ethanol or any other flammable liquid?
- Will you be using potentially harmful chemicals such as hydrogen peroxide, acids and alkalis, enzymes?

Ensure you point out possible dangers and then describe the procedures you will follow to minimise any risks posed by these.

This aspect is not assessed in this skill but it is assessed in Manipulative Skills.

Method

- This can be written as a set of instructions or more personally, in which case it should be written in the future tense since you are planning to do it.
- It must follow the correct sequence of steps, eg. do not say ' I will fit the bung to the boiling tube but first I will add the methylene blue'.
- Ensure all the controlled variables you listed are controlled.
- Ensure they are controlled in an appropriate and precise way. This is where the correct choice of apparatus and material is important. Look at the section on Uncertainties and Errors on pages 12 - 13.
- State precisely all measurements, timings and equipment to use.
- If you are using different solutions have sufficient apparatus to prevent cross contamination.
- Take care not to give inappropriate descriptions eg. 'I will control the temperature with a thermometer'. A thermometer can only measure temperature, not control it.
- 'Amount' is an often misused word so avoid using it. For example 'Collect the same amount of leaves'. This could mean mass or number, so state this. 'Collect the same number of leaves'.
- Avoid writing the Method as an essay as it is difficult to follow the steps. Use paragraphs or even a bullet point or numbered list.

Example 1
Here is a poor example of a list of Apparatus and Method with teacher's comments.
The student is investigating the effect of temperature on the rate of digestion of starch by amylase.

Apparatus
Test tubes
Syringes
Beaker
Starch
Amylase
Iodine

Teacher's comments
We are not told what size the syringes and beaker should be. Looking at the method we can guess but that is unsatisfactory. Neither the starch nor amylase are given concentrations or volumes. These are key variables to control. In fact, as written they could be the dry powders! Likewise iodine is a solution.

Method
Fill a test tube with 15ml of the starch solution.
Add 5ml enzyme.

Teacher's comments
Non SI units used.
'Fill' is an inaccurate word to use. The test tube is greater than 15cm^3 since more has to be added to it and therefore 15cm^3 will not 'fill' it.
What was used to measure the 15cm^3 and the 5cm^3?

Place the test tube in a beaker of warm water and measure the temperature.

'Warm' is a vague term. The student is making some attempt to control the temperature variable but it is too inaccurate. Do we measure the temperature of the starch-amylase mixture or the temperature of the water? The starch and amylase have already been mixed and so the temperature of the reaction mixture is going to change as it warms up.

Remove a sample of the reaction mixture after 30 seconds and add to a drop of iodine.

I haven't been told to start a stop watch so I cannot do this!! How big a sample? What is the iodine in? I haven't been told to prepare the iodine.

This clearly would gain 'Not at all'.

You should have the picture by now. There is a lack of accuracy, precision and detail so the assessment criteria are not being met.

Now look at Example 2 on the next page at how the student should have written the Apparatus list and Method.

Example 2

Apparatus
2 x boiling tubes
$20cm^3$ syringe
$5cm^3$ syringe
$500cm^3$ beaker
$300cm^3$ 10% starch solution
$100cm^3$ 2% amylase solution
stopwatch
thermometer
2 x fine ended dropping pipette
dimple tray
standard iodine solution
Bunsen burner, gauze, heat mat, matches
safety goggles
marker pen

Sizes of containers are stated.

SI units used.

Concentrations and volumes of solutions specified.

Precise description.

Number of this item required is specified.

Risk Assessment
The procedure uses an enzyme and iodine.
Wear safety goggles.

Risk Assessment included.

Method

Using a $20cm^3$ syringe measure $15cm^3$ of the starch solution into a labelled boiling tube. Using a $5cm^3$ syringe measure $5cm^3$ of the amylase solution into another labelled boiling tube.
Put approximately $400cm^3$ of tap water into a $500cm^3$ beaker. (The precise volume does not matter as this is only a water bath). Heat this to 30^0C with a Bunsen burner and monitor the temperature with a thermometer. Place both labelled boiling tubes in the water bath and wait till the temperatures of both solutions reach 30^0C.
Using a dropping pipette, carefully place 2 drops of iodine solution into each dimple of the dimple tile. When the solutions have reached the correct temperature pour the starch into the amylase and immediately start the stopwatch. After 15 seconds use a clean dropping pipette to remove a sample from the mixture and carefully place 2 drops into the first iodine drop on the dimple tile. Note the colour change.
Every 15 seconds take a fresh sample and continue this until there is no longer a colour change with the iodine.
Note the final temperature of the mixture.
Repeat the method to obtain two further consistent results. If the temperature of the solutions has dropped more than 2 degrees use the Bunsen burner to keep the temperature of the water bath up.

Appropriate equipment is used to ensure accuracy.

Apparatus labelled to avoid errors.

Appropriate measurements taken for reliability.

Careful use of equipment.

Repeats to ensure reliability.

Careful monitoring of a controlled variable.

This is not the complete method of course but it should give the idea of how it should be written. (I am assuming here that the student does not have access to a thermostatically controlled water bath. Clearly if it was available it should be used).

- Note how <u>all</u> the variables are being controlled as accurately as possible.
- Note also how the Method is broken into four paragraphs for different phases of the procedure. This improves the appearance and makes it more clear. Alternatively use a bullet point list.
- This has been written as a set of instructions like a recipe. The more personal format would be – I will use a $20cm^3$ syringe to measure $15cm^3$ of the starch solution ....

Section 1.2

Data Collection and Processing

Data Collection and Processing	Recording raw data	Processing raw data	Presenting processed data
Complete	Records appropriate quantitative and associated qualitative raw data, including units and uncertainties where relevant.	Processes the quantitative raw data correctly.	Presents processed data appropriately and, where relevant, includes errors and uncertainties.

Data collection and processing needs only one heading but may need a second.

- **Results and Analysis**
- **(Statistical formulae)**

Data

Data comes in two forms –

- raw data, and
- processed data.

If the raw data is extensive, such as with a correlation investigation, it is usually placed in an appendix at the end, and the "Results" section contains only the summary. If though the raw data is only brief then it can all be included in the Results section.

Raw data should still be clear, organised, and with headings and units. Remember to distinguish between your data and that from other students you have collected to add to yours.

Organising the Data

If raw data is put down as you collect it, it may be difficult to make sense of it so it needs to be organised. Look at the raw data below on the shell diameter of a sample of 22 limpets.

Shell diameter / mm ±0.5	9	19	25	23	8	19	20	13	23	27	12
Shell diameter / mm ±0.5	26	21	34	24	15	17	27	17	31	23	16

A brief search tells us that the smallest limpet had a shell diameter of 8mm, and the largest 34mm, though we still had to look carefully. If our sample was larger we could easily make a mistake by missing the smallest or largest. We should organise the data by ranking or ordering it, ie arrange them in ascending order.

Shell diameter / mm ±0.5	8	9	12	13	15	16	17	17	19	19	20
Shell diameter / mm ±0.5	21	23	23	23	24	25	26	27	27	31	34

Another way of organising might be grouping. Look at the raw data below on the lengths of a sample of 24 leaves.

Length / mm ± 0.5	105	93	122	98	103	112	114	127	103	107	121	99
Length / mm ± 0.5	91	115	102	106	115	124	108	97	111	113	118	107

This form of raw data could be grouped into classes as shown in the table on the right. Note that the classes are all of equal size and arranged in ascending order.

Leaf length / mm ±0.5	Number of leaves
90 – 94	2
95 – 99	3
100 – 104	3
105 – 109	5
110 – 114	4
115 – 119	3
120 – 124	3
125 – 129	1

Note the uncertainty is shown with a ± symbol. See page 12 for more information on uncertainty.

See page 57 for a tip on how to insert the ± symbol quickly using a keyboard shortcut.

Tabulating the Data

Each individual item of data is called a **value**.
Numerical data should always be tabulated and there are rules to follow.
Tables are easily drawn in word processors such as Microsoft Word. (All of this Guide is done in Word).

- Never split any table from one page to the next.
- Always centre the columns of data and align decimal points using a decimal tab.
- Never put more than one value in a row of a column.
- Tables are usually arranged vertically but sometimes can be arranged horizontally.
- In a vertical table the order of the columns must follow a logical sequence, ie the independent data column on the left and the values arranged in ascending order. The dependent variable(s) comes next.
- In a horizontal table the first row is the independent variable.
- The columns/rows must have precise headings and contain units written after the diagonal line. Be careful with minutes and seconds. You may measure a time as 5 minutes and 15 seconds, but if you put a column heading of minutes and then write 5.15, this is not 5 minutes 15 seconds but 5.15 minutes, which is actually 5 minutes and 9 seconds. Use either minutes OR seconds as appropriate.
- The column/row headings must be the same as the axis labels on the graph or graphs.
- Always include the uncertainty in the column heading after the units.
- Always use SI units (page 6) but only in the column/row heading and never with the values in the table.
- The number of decimal places for the values is important – see page 14.
  The number of decimal places can vary across columns, but all the values of a single column should be to the same number of decimal places, eg 1.23; 1.50.
- There must be an informative title. See the many examples in this Guide.
- If the table is hand drawn then the lines must be drawn with a ruler.

Note – Volume not Amount.

The usual type of table arranged vertically

Temperature of vitamin C solution / ^{0}C ± 0.5	Start reading on burette / cm^{3} ± 0.05	End reading on burette / cm^{3} ± 0.05	Volume of vitamin C used / cm^{3} ± 0.05
25	50.5	26.5	24.0
35	75.5	31.0	44.5

A horizontal table.

Pulse rate / beats min^{-1} ±1	60-64	65-69	70-74	75-79
Number of students	2	3	8	12

Below and on pages 12 and 15 are annotated examples of tables.

Here is an example of an organised raw data table.

These headings will also be the axis labels on the graph.

Title of each variable at the top of each column.

Units of measurement after the diagonal line.

Uncertainty

Temperature / ^{0}C ±0.5	Time taken to travel 10cm / s ±1
15	80
25	60
35	30
45	10

Units here - **not** here.

Concise and informative title.

Independent variable in first column, arranged in ascending order.

Dependent variable in succeeding column.

Data centred.

Table 1*. Results of the effect of changing temperature on the time taken for an air bubble to travel 10cm in a potometer with a cut shoot of ivy, *Hedera* sp.

*It is very helpful to put Table 1, Table 2, Graph 1, Graph 2 etc at the start of the title. This then allows you easily to refer to a particular table or graph in your Discussion or Evaluation.

The table may have double headings.

Dependent variables.

Independent variables. The cells have been merged.

SI units.

Uncertainty.

Student	Before exercise		At end of exercise	
	Pulse rate / beats min^{-1} ±2	Breathing rate/ breaths min^{-1} ±2	Pulse rate / beats min^{-1} ±2	Breathing rate/ breaths min^{-1} ±2
1	55	14	120	42
2	61	16	135	51

Table 1. Pulse and breathing rates of two students before and after exercise

Uncertainties and Errors – Limitations of Measurements

I prefer to use the term 'Uncertainty' as 'Error' implies you have made a mistake.

Whenever you collect data there will be uncertainties, or limitations of measurements, that you need to take into account. It is important because it will affect the reliability of your conclusion – if the uncertainties or limitations are large your conclusion could be in doubt. **Never** change or make up results to try and fit the pattern but instead discuss them in your Evaluation of Results.

- **The uncertainty must be included on your data tables (see page 11) and your graph (see page 16).**

There are different types of uncertainty –

- instrument uncertainties;
- estimated uncertainties;
- biological uncertainties;
- anomalous results.

Instrument Uncertainties

When dealing with apparatus there is a sensible limit as to how accurate a measurement should be. A thermometer can be read to 0.5^{0}C; a ruler can be read to 0.5 millimetres; a burette can be read to 0.05cm^3. However the uncertainty should be based on what is being measured.

Example: The length of a leaf could be measured at 45mm ± 1mm giving an acceptable error of 2.2%. On the other hand the width of the leaf could be measured at 5.5mm ± 0.5mm, giving an error of 9.1%. If we maintained the ±1mm for the width the error would double to 18.2%. This is less acceptable. This is why it is important to select carefully the measuring device – it would be very inaccurate to use a 250cm^3 measuring cylinder to measure 10cm^3.

Always use the most accurate apparatus available to you AND use it carefully and precisely. Some examples –

- Read off volume measuring equipment such as a burette from the bottom of the meniscus with your eye level with the meniscus;
- Ensure air bubbles are not trapped in a syringe and you know where to position the plunger;
- When measuring temperature stir the liquid and do not remove the thermometer from the liquid as the reading will drop rapidly;
- Electronic equipment such as colorimeters can 'drift' after being set. Always check the setting against the standard solution every so often and note any possible drifting.
- School electronic pH metres are generally not very accurate so test it in a buffer solution of known pH.

Estimated Uncertainties

When you are collecting observation data using living specimens it is often difficult to be precise or certain about a particular observation. Examples –

- gill movements of a fish;
- abdominal breathing movements of a locust;
- cirripedia movements of a barnacle;
- heart beats of Daphnia.

In such cases you should make a sensible estimated uncertainty. For example with the first two the uncertainty might be ±1 or perhaps 2. In the second two the uncertainty is likely to be much higher, especially the last one. The uncertainty can be different for different values of the independent variable.

Biological Uncertainties
Biological data will inevitably contain variation because organisms vary. You should be aware of this when selecting material for investigation and planning your variables. You can reduce uncertainties by –

- having a large sample. A sample size of less than 5 is of little value. If you wish to do a statistical analysis aim for a minimum sample size of 7 and ideally at least 15;
- random sampling;
- selecting similar organisms or biological material, eg.
  - for behaviour investigations with woodlice make sure all the specimens are of the same species;
  - for osmosis or catalase investigations with potatoes make sure all the samples come from the same potato.
- having sufficient repeats to obtain at least two consistent readings – see page 16.

Anomalous Results

These are values that do not fit the general pattern or trend, or do not fit the predicted line on a graph.

- Do not include them in calculations, eg the mean and standard deviation from a set of repeats.
- If you have obtained the values by calculation, check that you have not made a mathematical error.

Look at these three examples.

Volume of gas collected in 60 seconds / cm^3 ±0.05
5
6
5
9 *
4
5

Table 1.

Volume of CO_2 released / cm^3 ±0.05
0.1
0.5 *
0.0
0.0
0.1
0.0

Table 2.

Resting pulse rates of 6 students / beats.min^{-1} ±1
76
77
50 *
72
68
69

Table 3

* indicates values that you might consider to be anomalous.

In Table 1 the 9 does not appear to fit the general pattern but don't be too hasty. Always include such raw data though and mark it in some way, eg with an *, and then discuss it in the Evaluation of Results.

Now let's look more carefully at this value of 9 before we dismiss it as anomalous. What we must do is calculate the mean and standard deviation, <u>including</u> the suspect value. (This is easily done in an Excel spreadsheet – see page 19). This is shown on the table on the right. We find that the value of 9 lies within +2 standard deviations of the mean (5.7 + (2 x 1.8) = 9.3) and we can accept this, so we would have been wrong to dismiss it as anomalous.

	Volume of gas collected in 60 seconds / cm^3 ±0.05
1	5.0
2	6.0
3	5.0
4	9.0
5	4.0
6	5.0
mean	5.7
standard deviation	1.8

Now look at Table 2. If we again calculate the mean (0.12) and the standard deviation (0.19) we find that the value of 0.5 is exactly +2 standard deviations and we could reasonably consider it as an anomaly. We therefore need to recalculate both mean and standard deviation excluding this value.

What about the 50 beats though in Table 3? Remember that biological data is highly variable and it is important not to accuse a certain result as being anomalous unless you are certain and have a big enough sample to show that it is. In this case we find the mean is 72.4 beats and the standard deviation is 4.0 beats, which does indeed make the value of 50 beats outside -2 standard deviations from the mean. Therefore you could consider the 50 beats to be 'anomalous' in this particular sample, but given the data being collected the sample is clearly far too small. In an appropriately large sample you would probably find that the value of 50 beats was at the lower end of a normal distribution.

Processing the Data

The type of processing depends on what the data is, what you are investigating, and what you are trying to find out. Processing may be numerical, graphical, or both. Simple numerical and statistical processing is dealt with below, and more complex statistics in Sections 1.4 and 1.4.1. Graphs are dealt with in Section 1.2.1.

Clearly it is much easier to do this processing in a word processor such as Word, or a spreadsheet such as Excel. Tables in Word can do simple things such as calculating mean and sorting, but it is often easier to embed an Excel spreadsheet into your Word document. The spreadsheet can then be used to do all the calculations such as standard deviation, and draw a graph. There is information on embedding an Excel spreadsheet on page 25 and plotting graphs in Excel on page 21.

The very simplest form of processing is calculating some form of average, usually the **mean**. If time is involved we may want to calculate **rate**. To look at the spread of our data we would calculate **standard deviation**, which is a very simple and useful statistic, or perhaps standard error of the mean.

Significant Figures and Decimal Places

When processing think about significant figures and decimal places, and be sensible. It would be rather stupid to present the mean time taken to collect 1cm^3 of oxygen from a catalase experiment as 72.37534 seconds, even though that is what it said on your calculator. 72 seconds would be appropriate here. A useful guideline is to use the standard deviation value if you have calculated it. Take this to 2 significant figures and do not have more than the same number of decimal places for the mean.

Examples - Standard deviation = 34mm (2sf and no dp); mean = 127mm (no dp).
Standard deviation = 1.0mm (2sf and one dp); mean = 5.8mm (one dp).

- Always use a full stop for the decimal and not a comma.

Averages

The term average is often used when talking about samples. There are three ways of measuring the average – **mean, median, and mode**. Which one is used depends on what you want to do with the data. Remember though to exclude any values that you consider to be anomalous, but you need to justify this – see previous page.

Calculating the Mean

The mathematical symbols used have been standardised.
Each measurement or value from a sample is given the symbol *x*.
The sum of all measurements is written as $\sum x$. ($\sum$ is the Greek letter sigma).

The number of values in the sample is n.
The mean of the sample is x-bar, $\bar{x}$

The mean = sum of all samples / sample size

$$\bar{x} = \frac{\sum x}{n}$$

Calculating the Median

This is the middle number for the results when arranged in rank order. (Remember median has a d (nearly) in the middle, or alternatively they both have the same number of letters).

Calculating the Mode

This is the measurement that occurs the greatest number of times. (Remember m**o**de and m**o**st).

- Most of the time you are calculating the **mean** and so use this word rather than average.

Take the following set of results obtained from measuring the width of 10 beech leaves.

Raw data.

Sample	Leaf width / cm ±0.5
1	1.6
2	1.4
3	1.7
4	1.4
5	1.4
6	2.0
7	1.2
8	1.6
9	1.8
10	1.5

Note the use of 0 to give the same number of decimal places.

The same data but sorted into ascending rank order.

	Leaf width / cm ±0.5
	1.2
	1.4
	1.4
	1.4
	1.5
	1.6
	1.6
	1.7
	1.8
	2.0
mean	1.56
median	1.55
mode	1.4

Since there is an even number of samples the median is the mean between the fifth and sixth values when arranged in rank order.

A decimal tab has been used to align all the numbers.

Further Calculations

Calculating the mean is simple and the formula used need not be included. However for other calculations, including statistics, you need to state the formula and the method used - calculator, specific statistics software or a spreadsheet such as Excel. See the statistical formulae section on pages 54 – 56 for commonly used formulae.

- All calculations and formulae must have a clear heading.

Calculating a Rate

Rate is how fast something is happening in unit time. For example you may be collecting gas given off from a reaction. The rate is given by –

$$\frac{\text{volume of gas given off}}{\text{time for volume to be given off}}$$

Rate can also be determined from a graph when time is the dependent variable. The rate at time t is the gradient of the tangent of the graph at this point.

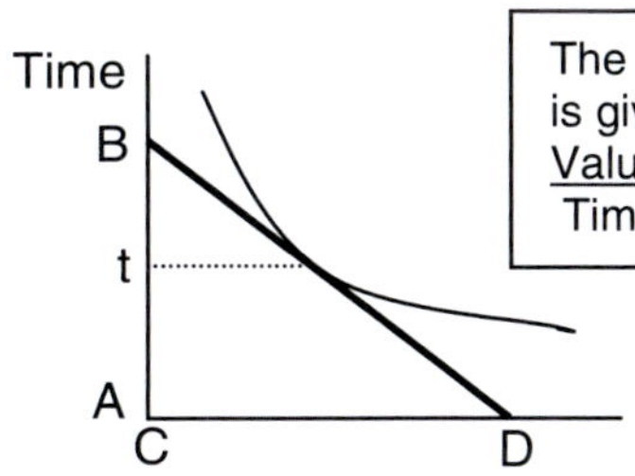

The gradient at time t is given by $\frac{\text{Value CD}}{\text{Time AB}}$

Putting Processed Data into a Table

Some processing can be carried out on the table by adding appropriate columns and rows. Do it if you can rather than in separate tables or lines of writing.

Title of each variable at the top of each column.

Units of measurement after the diagonal line.

Uncertainty included.

Data processed in table.

SI units.

Temperature / ^{0}C ±0.5	Time taken to travel 10cm / s ±1	Rate of uptake / cm s^{-1}
15	80	0.8
25	60	0.6
35	30	0.3
45	10	0.1

Independent variable in first column, arranged in ascending order.

Dependent variable in succeeding column.

Data centred.

Decimal points in line.

Always use a full stop for the decimal point and NOT a comma.

Table 1. Results of the effect of changing temperature on the rate of water uptake in a cut shoot of ivy, *Hedera* sp.

Concise and informative title. Compare this to the one on page 11.

Including Uncertainty on a Graph

See pages 26 - 28 for how to plot uncertainty bars using Excel. (Excel calls them error bars).

Example 1

Suppose you collected the following data. You decided the uncertainty in your measuring was ±2.0cm^3.

Temperature / ^{0}C	Volume of gas collected / cm^3, ± 2.0
5	26
10	39
15	44
20	51
25	55

The points look rather uneven but you can still draw a smooth curve through the uncertainty values. I have used Excel to plot the uncertainty bars but used the curved line drawing tool in Word to draw the line exactly where I want it.

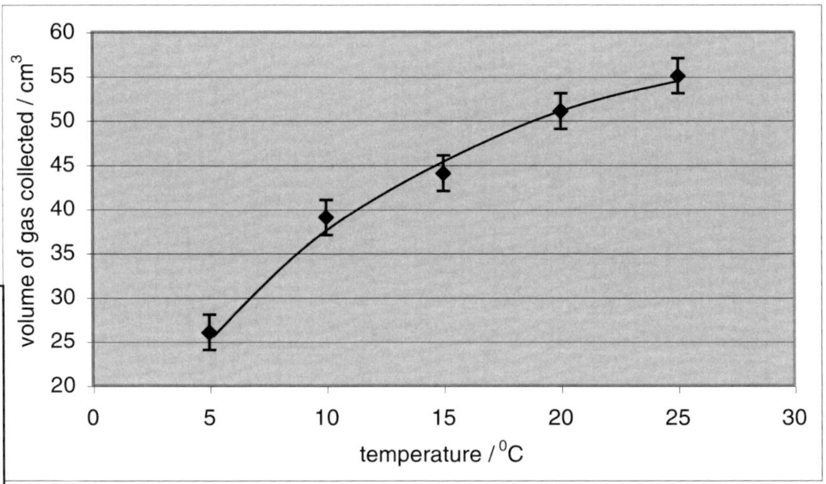

Graph 1. Effect of temperature on volume of gas collected.

The uncertainty does not need to be the same for every reading. In the above example you may feel that when the gas production was slow at the lower temperatures the uncertainty was small, maybe ±0.5cm^3, but at the high temperatures the uncertainty was greater at ±2cm^3. More on this on page 28.

Example 2

A student collected the following raw data.

Temperature of reaction / ^{0}C	Repeats for times taken for iodine solution to lose blue colour / s	
	1	2
15	24	23

Here the two readings are very similar and so she decides not to take a further repeat. She plots the mean, 23.5s, with the uncertainty bar from 24s to 23s which shows the spread of the values.

Example 3

Temperature of reaction / ^{0}C	Repeats for times taken for iodine solution to lose blue colour / s			
	1	2	3	4
20	24	22	25	23

Here she took further readings because there is some variation. However they are similar and so she plots the mean 23.5s with the uncertainty bar from 25s to 22s, again showing the spread of values.

Example 4

Temperature of reaction / ^{0}C	Repeats for times taken for iodine solution to lose blue colour / s			
	1	2	3	4
25	24	15*	22	23

Here the first and second readings are very different so she has taken two further readings to confirm. She does not have enough values to calculate standard deviation, decides the 15s is anomalous and so ignores it when calculating the mean. She plots the mean of 23.0s with the uncertainty bar from 24s to 22s.The 15 is marked with * and commented on.

In Examples 2, 3 and 4 we have assumed that there is no other form of uncertainty. The student may decide though that there is an estimated uncertainty of 4s because she is not absolutely sure when the iodine has actually lost the blue colour. She would then add 2s each to the top and bottom of her uncertainty bars. Taking Example 4 the uncertainty bar goes from 20 to 26s and would look like this on the graph.

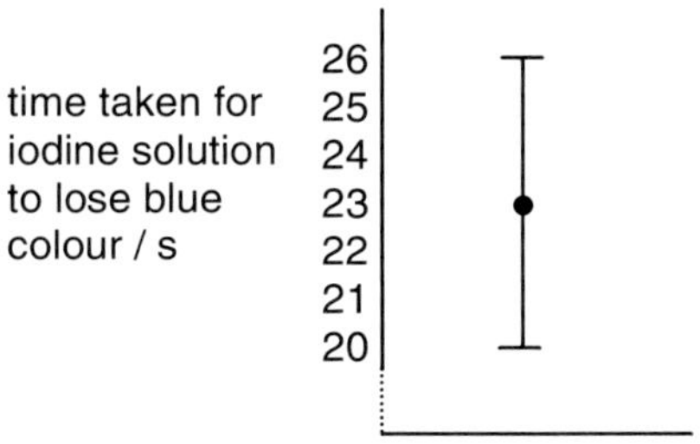

So far we have only considered uncertainty related to the dependent variable. However the independent variable may also have an uncertainty. On the previous page temperature would have an uncertainty of $\pm 0.5^0C$.

For example let us take an investigation where we are looking at the effect of glucose concentration on the rate of respiration in yeast. The teacher provides us with glucose solutions of 5%, 10%, 15%, 20% and 25%. We can accept these percentages with no uncertainty simply because the teacher or technician has made them up and we can assume they are accurate, so we only need plot an uncertainty for the dependent variable.

But what if you are designing the investigation and are simply provided with a 50% glucose solution? Now you have to make your own dilutions by measuring out volumes of distilled water and glucose solution and this of course is where error can creep in. You may use syringes and they are accurate, but you may decide that there is an uncertainty of $0.05cm^3$ when you measure the water and the same when you measure the glucose solution giving you $0.1cm^3$ overall. You are using $10cm^3$ of glucose solution so this is an uncertainty of ±1%. This will also need to be plotted.

Note use of the word Mean and not Average.

Here are some results.

Concentration of glucose solution / % ±1	Volume of carbon dioxide released / cm^3 ±0.2				
	Trial 1	2	3	4	Mean
5	2.1	2.5	2.3	2.1	2.25
10	4.5	4.5	4.8	4.6	4.60
15	8.4	8.4	8.6	8.6	8.50
20	9.7	9.4	9.3	9.6	9.50
25	7.0	7.3	7.4	7.1	7.20

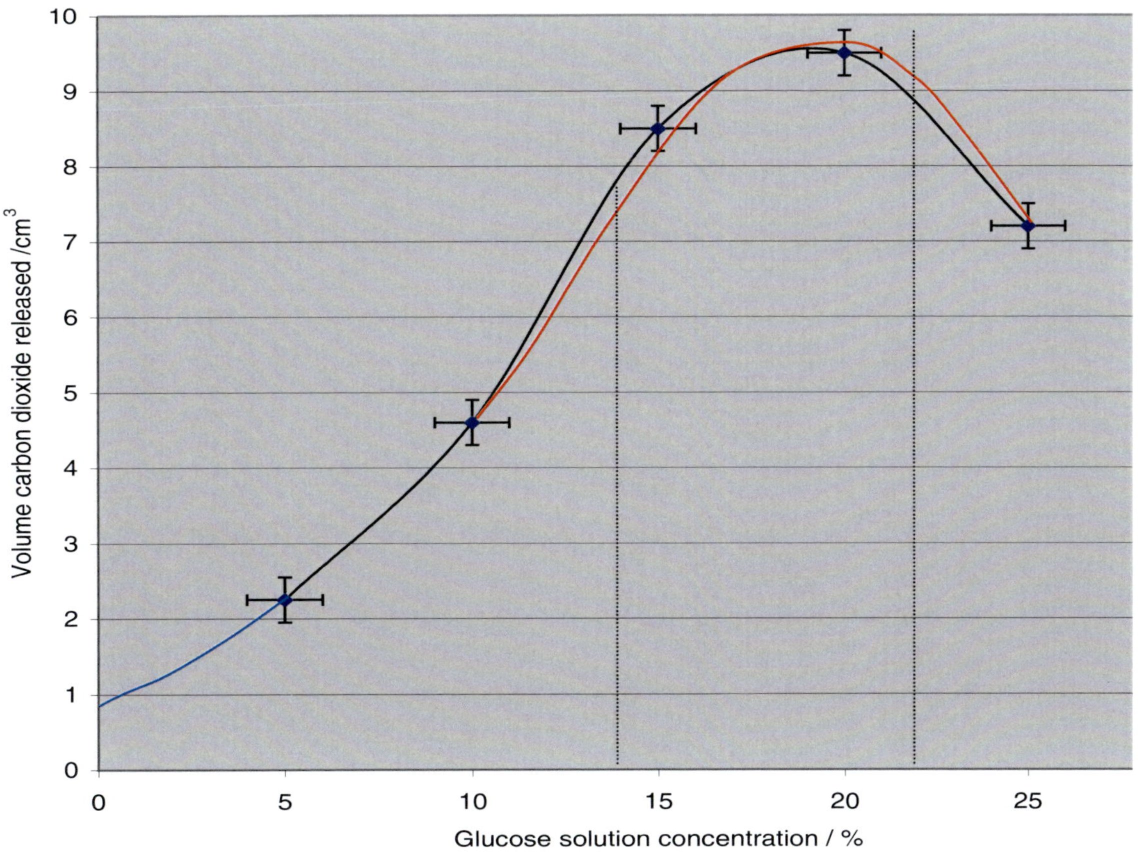

Graph 1. The effect of changing glucose concentration on the volume of carbon dioxide released during yeast fermentation.

Excel has drawn the black line but if I extrapolate it back to 0% glucose (blue line) I seem to get nearly $1cm^3$ of carbon dioxide released whereas I might think it should be $0cm^3$ given that the yeast is in water. Clearly my design is poor – I forgot to include a control of 0% glucose!

Now look at the red line. I have decided that I can draw this slightly different line that is still within my X and Y uncertainty bars. How do I find out which is better? I would need to do some intermediate glucose concentrations, perhaps 14% and 22% as shown by the dotted lines.

Standard Deviation

This analysis measures the spread or variability of your data – a small value for standard deviation indicates that your data is close to the mean, and a large value indicates that it is spread out. For an <u>experiment</u> the smaller the standard deviation the more reliable your mean will be.
If you are looking at the standard deviation of just one set of values then how do you decide whether it is 'small' or 'large'?

- If the standard deviation is greater than 33% of the mean then you can call that large.

The larger your sample is the better. You should not calculate standard deviation if you have less than 5 values.

The standard rule is that in a normal distribution 68% of the data falls within + or – one standard deviation of the mean, and 95% falls within + or – two standard deviations.

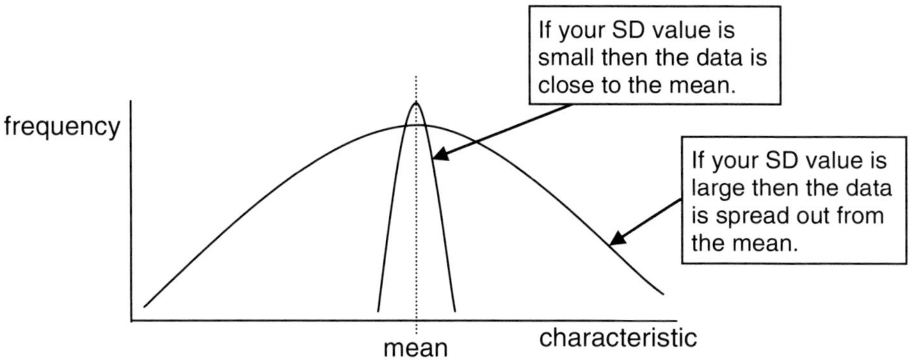

<u>Example</u>

Let us say the mean is 30 seconds and the standard deviation is 5 seconds.

68% of the values will fall within the times of 25 to 35 seconds, and 95% of the values will fall within the times of 20 to 40 seconds.

An alternative to standard deviation is standard error of the mean. This is looking at your data in a slightly different way but it can be useful for more detailed analysis for say an Extended Essay. See page 58.

Checking for Normal Distribution

For some data you can do a tally chart to check for normal distribution.

Note that the numbers for the independent variable are consecutive even though there may be zero values, as with 68 and 70 in the table.

Pulse rate / beats min^{-1}	Number of pupils
65	|
66	|||
67	|
68	
69	||
70	
71	||||||

Clearly this is not a normal distribution, probably because the sample is too small.

This distribution is very slightly skewed, but it is good enough.

This is a good normal distribution.

Size class of leaf length / cm	Shaded site	Sunny site
2.5 – 3.0		||
3.0 – 3.5		||||| |
3.5 – 4.0	||	||||| ||||
4.0 – 4.5	||||	||||
4.5 – 5.0	||||| ||	||
5.0 – 5.5	||||	
5.5 – 6.0	|	
6.0 – 6.5	|	
6.5 – 7.0	|	

Calculating Standard Deviation

The symbol for standard deviation is **s** or sometimes σ. There are different formulae that can be used depending on the data that you have collected. The ones normally used are on page 54. Sometimes you can group your data into frequencies and use the frequency formula.

- You need to learn how to calculate standard deviation using your calculator.
- Remember that standard deviation has the same units as the data values and so must be in the column heading in a table.

When using your Ti84 calculator (or another one in the Ti series) to find standard deviation for a sample it will give you two possible standard deviations. Always choose the larger one as this uses n-1 rather than n. Likewise with other calculators if there is a key $\sigma_{n\text{-}1}$ or $s_{n\text{-}1}$ then use that in preference to σ_n or s_n.

This is how to use an Excel spreadsheet. Excel uses the formulae on page 54. See also page 29.

	Data set 1	Data set 2
	16	41
	18	45
	19	81
	15	86
	15	99
	17	60
	18	58
Mean	16.9	67
St. dev.	1.6	22

1.6 is small relative to the mean of 16.9 (9.5%).

22 is also small relative to the mean of 67 (32.8%).

For the mean place cursor in cell below set of data;
Click Formulas;
Click More Functions;
Click Statistical;
Click AVERAGE;
Check the selected cells are correct;
Click OK.

For standard deviation place cursor in cell below mean;
Click Formulas;
Click More Functions;
Click Statistical;
Click STDEV.S;
Select the cells (make sure the mean is not included);
Click OK;

When you have done this for the first time Excel remembers these and lists them under Recently Used on the Formulas ribbon.

Correct the number of decimal places. (See page 14).
Select the cells with the mean and standard deviations;
On the Home ribbon go to General and expand the box.
The Format Cells window appears.
Click Number;
Choose 1 or 2 decimal places as appropriate;
Click OK.

- If you are using standard deviation to compare the spread of data then simply look at the relative percentage values. In this example 32.8% is clearly very much bigger than 9.5%.

- Let's look more critically at these two standard deviation values. They are both less than 33% of the mean but the second one is only just less. This would mean that the data is actually quite spread out – another 0.2% and it would be considered large. These are points that need to be considered in your Evaluation of Results.

Section 1.2.1

Graphical Presentation

Why use graphical presentation?
The role of a graph is to provide a quick visual relationship between the numerical data that is not always apparent from the data table. A graph also shows more clearly the relationship between two or more sets of data, and compliments any numerical analysis.

Types of Graph

The usual types of graphical presentation you will use are –

- Line graph,
- Scatter graph,
- Bar graph,
- Histogram,
- Pie chart,
- Kite diagram.

> Excel uses different terms.
> • For plotting line and scatter graphs use 'Scatter' and not 'Line'.
> • For bar graphs use either 'Column' or 'Bar', usually the 'Clustered' version.
> • For histograms use 'Column / Clustered'.

There are a number of other forms of data presentation. For details of these look in Skills in Advanced Biology 1 – Dealing with Data by J.W.Garvin. (Stanley Thornes Publishers). Your School or Biology Library may have a copy.

Which one do I use?

This depends on the type of data you have collected.

- Line graphs are used when you have carried out an experiment with dependent and independent variables. (A logarithmic graph could be used if you are investigating a rate.)
- Scatter graphs are used when you want to see if there is a correlation between two sets of data, neither of which has been manipulated.
- Bar graphs and histograms are similar in appearance but distinct in use.
  - A bar graph is used when there is no relationship between the bars and so there is a gap between them.
  - A histogram is used when each bar is directly related to the ones on each side of it and so there is no gap. It shows a distribution pattern which may be random, normal, or have a positive or negative skew.
- Pie charts are useful to show proportions of the whole and are often used in an ecological study.
- Kite diagrams show the distribution across a region and are also often used in an ecological study.

Simple and Compound Graphs

Compound graphs are when two or more sets of data are plotted on the same axes. If you are comparing the data then it is <u>essential</u> that they are together, but if there is no comparison then putting them together can cause confusion.
An example of a compound graph would be the effect of pH on the activity of the enzymes amylase and pepsin.

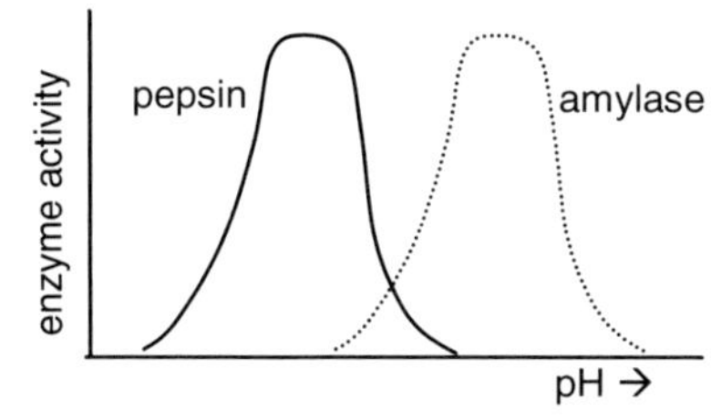

Three axes?

This is a form of compound graph where the sets of data are related but have different dependent scales. For example we can measure the volume of oxygen produced by a photosynthesising plant against wavelength of light.
We can then extract the chloroplast pigments and measure the % light absorption against wavelength of light. If we plot these two sets of data as a compound graph we can see if there is any relationship between the light absorption and the production of oxygen.

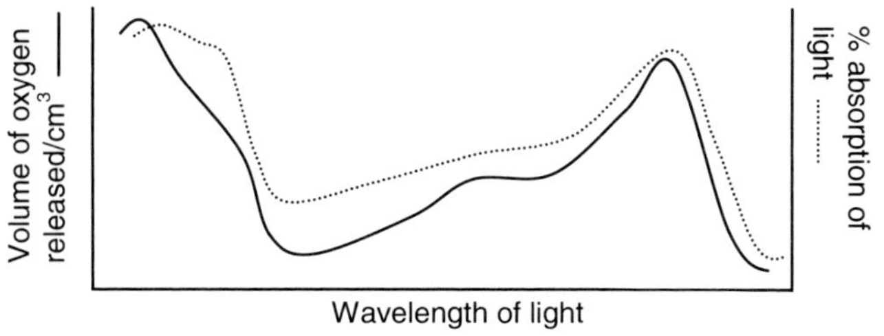

Which Data do I Plot?

In general you should use the processed data, often the mean, as your dependent variable on the Y-axis. Sometimes the data can be displayed in different ways as in the example below.

> If you investigated the effect of insulation on the effect of water cooling in a test tube, the independent variable would be the number of layers of insulation. You could present two types of graph as shown below. The first graph, the scattergraph, represents the cooling data, and the second one, the bar graph, represents the data after further processing.

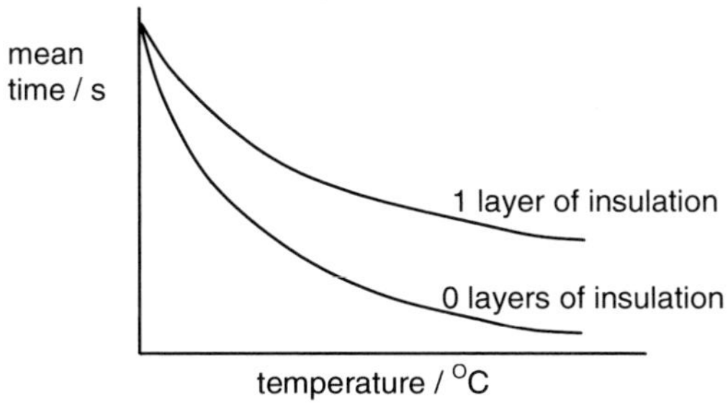

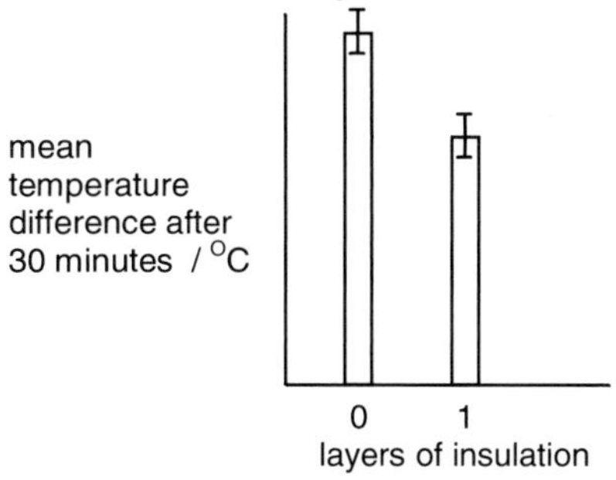

General Rules for Graphs

1. Excel works very well but it takes a little while to get to know how to use it well. Save the graph to a separate page so that it is large – see page 23 for an example.
2. If plotting by hand always use graph paper.
3. The paper can be rotated to portrait or landscape to create the best scales.
4. The dependent variable is **always** on the Y-axis.
5. The independent variable is **always** on the X-axis. (Remember X goes a-cross).
6. The scale does not have to start at zero. Rarely do you have to extrapolate in biological graphs, so select the scale to maximise the graph.
7. Scale divisions should be simple, 1, 2, 5 times a power of 10.
8. Always position the scale to allow space to label the axes. A rough guide on an A4 sheet of graph paper would be 2cm up and 3cm in from the left.
9. Plotting the points by hand. Use the co-ordinates to mark the point and then surround it with a small neat circle. ⊙ This is preferable to an x as this tends to obscure the actual point. Furthermore, if plotting a compound graph then the points can be surrounded with a circle, square or triangle. Excel does not allow you to do this, but it does allow you to change the styles and colours of the points and lines. If adding uncertainty bars then leave out the circle but make the actual point clear.
10. Label the axes with exactly the same titles as you used for the column headings in the data table.
11. Title the graph fully and precisely – see the many examples in this Guide.

Plotting Graphs in Excel

> **Warning**. *At the time of writing this (February 2013) there is an error in the 2010 software that causes Excel to crash and your computer to freeze just at the end of adding error bars, but only when it is embedded in a Word document. This means that at the moment you would need to do all your processing on a separate Excel document and then when complete paste it into your practical write-up in Word. This is annoying until Microsoft fix the error, but it does the job. However this problem does not occur in the 2007 version.*

It is important that the graph is -

- large;
- has the axes labelled with the same labels as used in the data table column headings;
- has a clear and precise title.

I suggest, as with the data tables, you have in the title Graph 1 / Graph 2. This makes it easy to refer to it in the Evaluation of Results.

❖ Do I include the column headings?

This depends on whether you have just one dependent variable or more than one.

- If you have just one then the answer is no.
- If you have more than one then the answer is yes.

Plotting the graph

Put your raw data into your data table, copy and paste it into the Excel spreadsheet and carry out the necessary processing.
Select the column containing your independent data values. (This should be column A).
Hold down the control key and select the column of your dependent data values that you wish to plot. This is probably your mean values.
From the ribbon select Insert.
Select the form of graph you want. Remember to use Scatter for both line and scattergraphs.
Your graph (chart) appears but with either Series1 or the legend on the right depending on whether you included the column heading in your selection. If it says Series1 right click on this and delete. If it is the legend then see below.
Select Chart Tools.
Select Design.
On right end of ribbon select Move Chart.
Select New Sheet.
Click OK.

You can now modify your graph on Chart1 and the data is still available on Sheet1.

Modify the X and Y scales if required by right clicking on an axis and selecting Format Axis. The Axis Options window appears. You will usually want the first of the Axis Options, the minimum value. Select Fixed and then type in the number.
The example below, which came from the data on page 24, illustrates this.

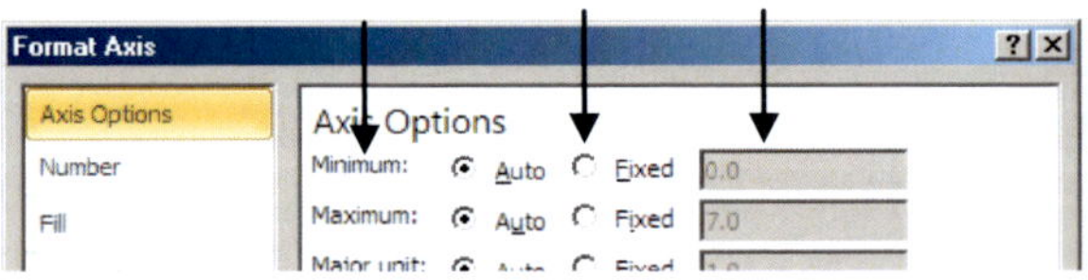

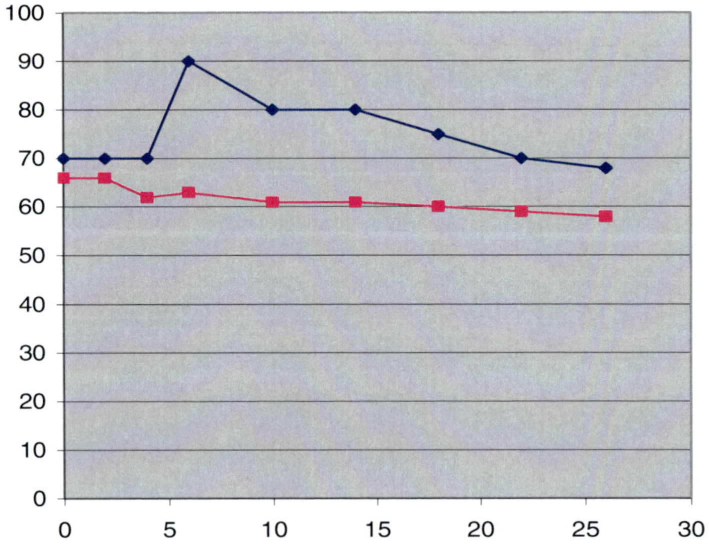

The horizontal scale is fine but the vertical scale clearly is not with the huge gap between 0 and 50 so this needs to be changed to a minimum value of 50.

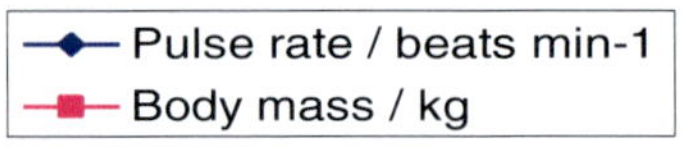

What else needs doing?
The axes do not have labels nor is there a title. However these will be added once you have embedded the graph into your write-up in Word.
In this example I have chosen to select the column headings so I have the legend.
Right click to select the box containing both and use the upper window to change the font and size to the same as you are using in your write-up. (I have a preference for this one which is Arial 10).
However can you see a problem with this legend? The label is min-1 and not min $^{-1}$. Unfortunately you cannot change this so after you have embedded the graph in your Word write-up simply put beats min^{-1} in a text box over the top.

I find the default lines rather thick but it is easy to change this.
Right click on the line and from the window select the drop-down for the line.
Hover over Weight and select 1pt.

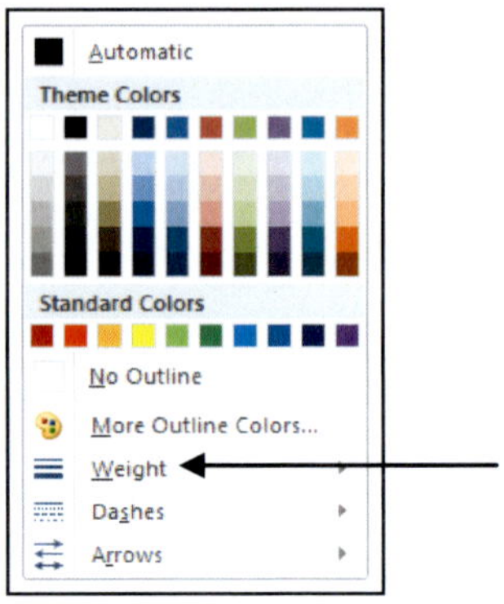

The graph below shows the final version having done all of the changes described above.

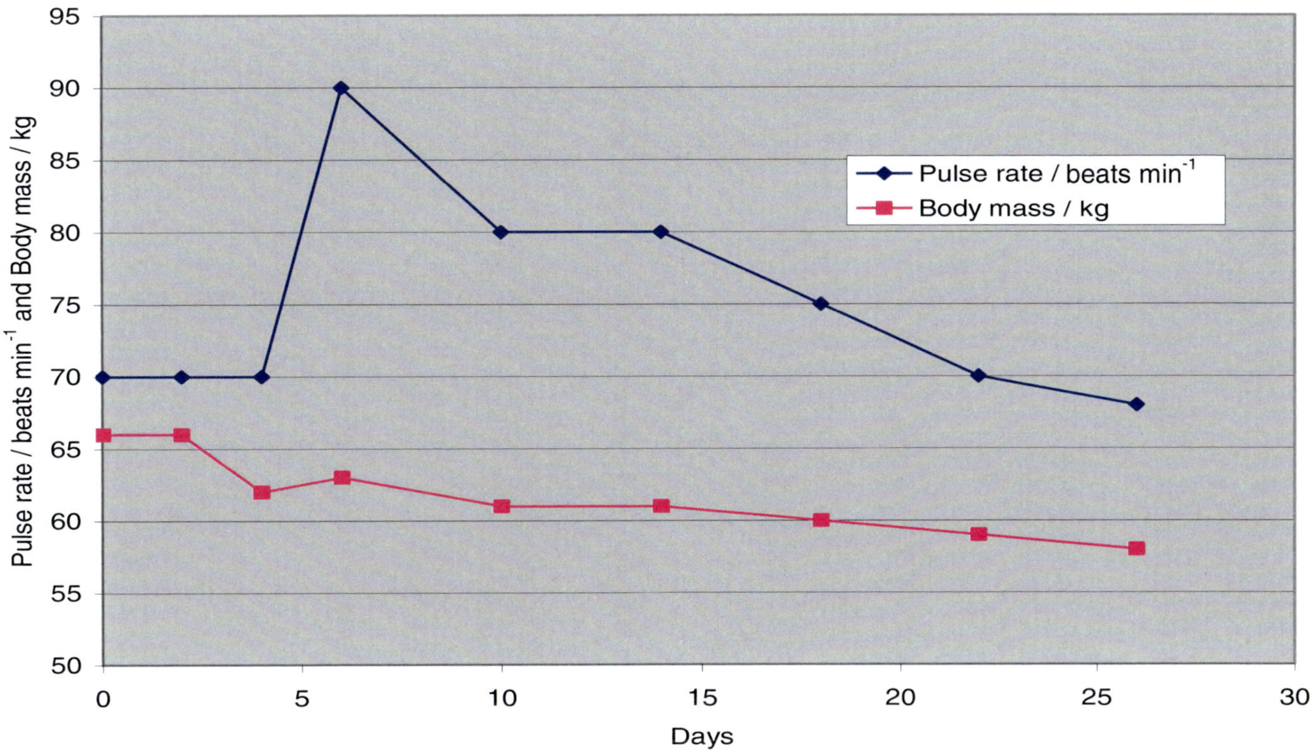

Graph 1. Pulse rate and body mass of patient over 26 day trial period.

Line Graphs and Scattergraphs

These are perhaps the most common type of graph that you will use.
Joining the points often causes problems.

- Should there be straight lines between the points?
- Or a line of best fit?
- Is the line of best fit a straight line or a curve?

Which you do depends on the relationship between the points. From your background information you might be expecting a straight line or curve because there is direct relationship between the points. Occasionally the points can be joined using ruled lines – see the example on the next page.
When you are drawing a curve by hand, rotate the paper so as to use the natural curving rotation of the wrist. Sometimes with Excel you may have to plot just the points and draw the line by hand or using the curve drawing tool in Word. The line on the graph on page 16 is an example of this.

- Remember that a line of best fit uses the uncertainty bars not the plotted values – see the graph on page 25.
- The line should pass through as many uncertainty bars as possible, and certainly two thirds of them.

The following two examples use Excel worksheets.

Example 1

Day	Pulse rate / beats min^{-1}	Body mass / kg
0	70	66
2	70	66
4	70	62
6	90	63
10	80	61
14	80	61
18	75	60
22	70	59
26	68	58

Table 1. Pulse rates and body mass of patient measured over a period of 26 days.

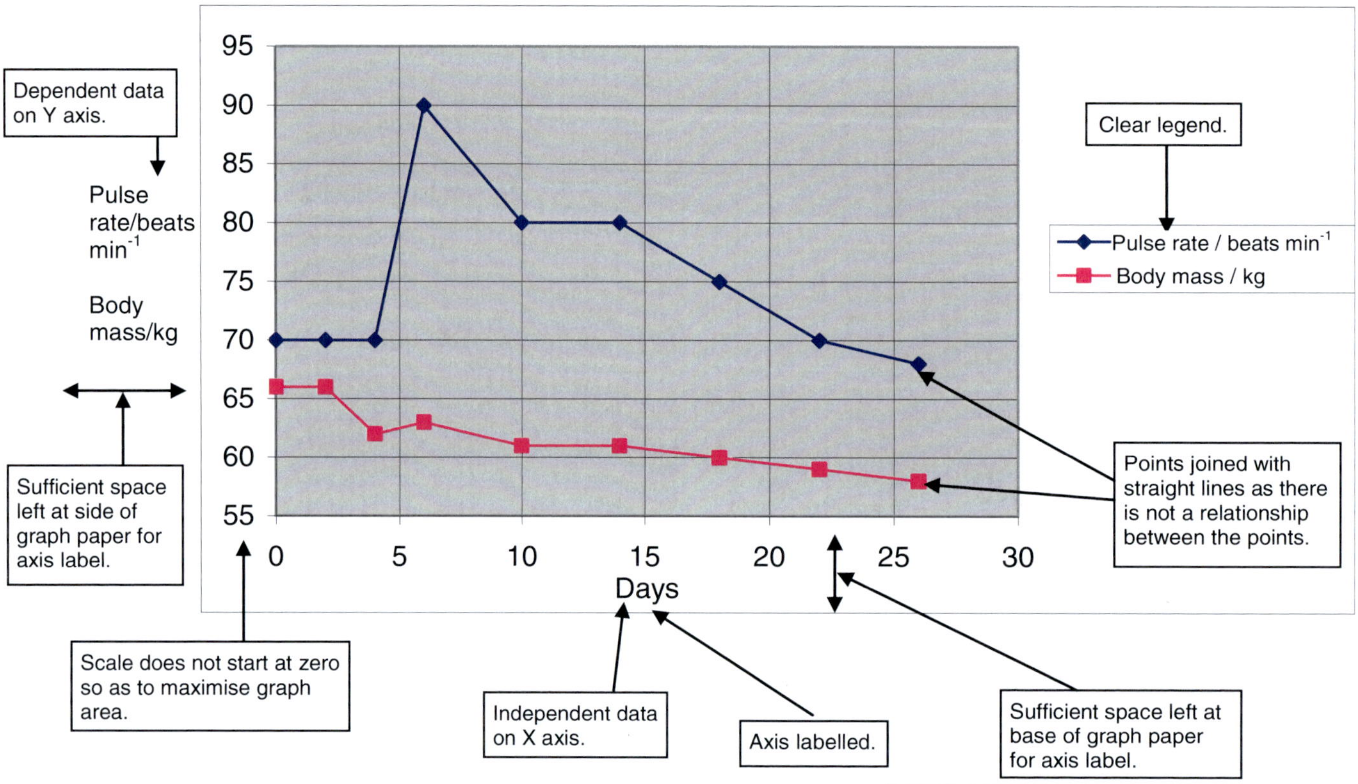

Graph 1. Pulse rate and body mass of patient over 26 day period.

In this compound graph one Y axis has the same scale for both sets of data. However, if the scales are different a second Y axis on the right hand side must be used.

The above graph is called a jagged line graph. It is used when you do not need to read off accurate values between the plotted data points and it is therefore not necessary to go to the trouble of joining the points by smooth curved lines.

Example 2

A student was investigating the synthesis of starch using glucose 1-phosphate as the substrate, along with an enzyme extracted from mung beans. The reaction mixture was kept in a water bath at 35°C and samples extracted at timed intervals. The sample was mixed with a fixed quantity of iodine in a colorimeter tube and the % transmission measured. As the reaction progressed the iodine mixture became darker as more starch was produced. The student predicted that the reaction would level off when all the substrate was used up.

time / s	0	10	20	30	40	50	60	70	80	90	100	110
% transmission ± 4	100	58	38	31	19	18	11	7	8	5	8	5

Table 1. Colorimeter readings of % transmission against time.

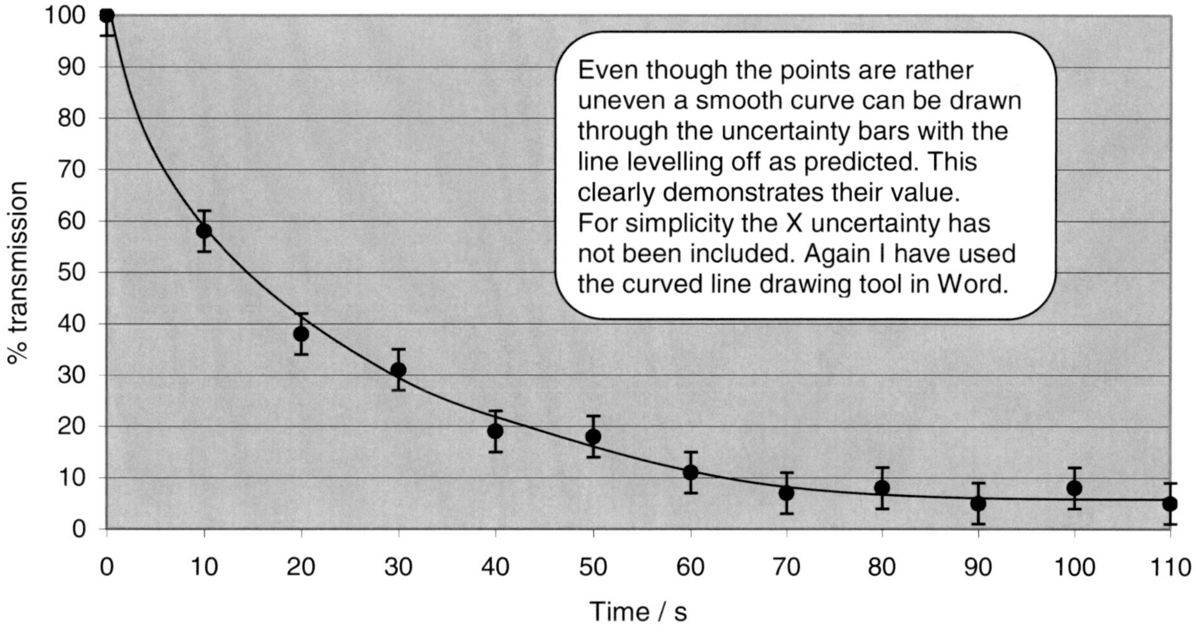

Graph 1. Colorimeter readings of % transmission against time.

Embedding an Excel spreadsheet into Word

It is much better to have the graphs as part of the text rather than separate sheets. If you embed an Excel spreadsheet then it becomes part of the Word document and you can add text before it easily if you need to and you can add your own line for the graph as well using the Word drawing tools.
Remember though that graphs must be large so that they are clear.
Set up your Word data table that will contain your processed data first and then the graph will appear below it. Word tables are easier to manipulate than Excel tables.
Because of the 2010 software problem you will need to keep the Excel spreadsheet separate and then paste it in once the data processing and graph have been done.
The Excel data table won't be visible as your actual data table will be the Word one. If you do a small graph and then expand it later all the words and numbers expand as well and it looks a mess!
To switch back to your Word document simply left click anywhere in the document.
To switch back to the Excel spreadsheet double left click anywhere on the Excel area.
Use Excel to do all the calculations for you and then transfer the processed data to the Word table – see pages 26 to 27.

Plotting Uncertainty Bars (Excel calls them error bars).

Uncertainty bars can be a bit of a problem but they need not be as Excel is very versatile and can do all the calculations and plotting for you if you know how to use it.
Remember that sometimes both X and Y uncertainty bars need to be plotted as shown on the graph on page 17.
Sometimes your uncertainty bars will have the same value for every point such as on the graph on page 25. Often they will not and this is where a little more needs to be done.
Note that all of the three procedures can be done on bar graphs as well. See page 31 for an example.

Are all my uncertainty bars the same value?

Go to subsection 1
Uncertainty bars with the same value.

Are my uncertainty bars with different values?

Go to subsection 2
Plotting maximum and minimum.

Go to subsection 3
Uncertainty bars with different values.

1. Uncertainty bars with the same value
On the ribbon select Chart Tools and Layout.
Click on Error Bars, then More Error Bar Options. Error bars will appear on your graph but ignore this.
The Format Error Bars appears with the Vertical Error Bars by default. Also by default the Both circle, the End Style Cap and Fixed Value are checked.
Type in the Fixed Value you want and click Close.

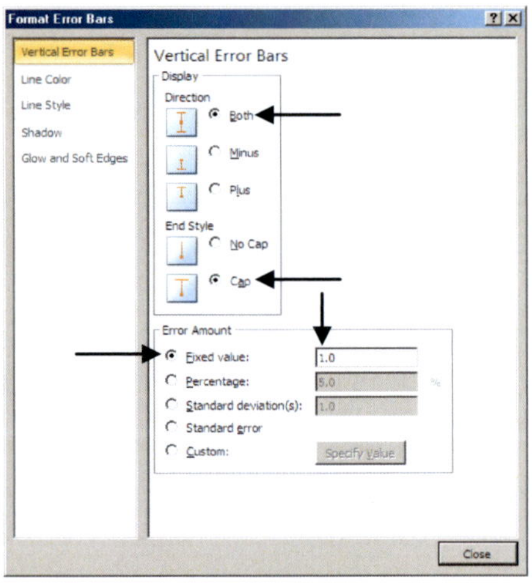

The Y error bars should now be on your graph but also oddly enough there are X (horizontal) error bars that Excel has decided to add for fun. If you don't want X error bars right click on any one and click Delete. However if you do, right click on any one and select Format Error Bars. The Horizontal Error Bars window appears. You can now follow the same procedure as before

2. Plotting maximum and minimum
You would normally do this if you only have 2 to 4 values for each data point.

Suppose you are investigating the effect of concentration of hydrogen peroxide on the release of oxygen by catalase and you have collected the data in the following table in your Word document. Note for simplicity I have included only three values for the independent variable – in a real investigation you should have at least six.

Hydrogen peroxide concentration / %	Volume of oxygen collected / cm^3			
	Set 1	Set 2	Set 3	Mean
50	13	12	15	
70	16	15	19	
100	27	29	28	

Note use of the word Mean and not Average.

Try doing these examples for practice.

Copy and paste these on to your Excel spreadsheet. Remember that this is not going to be visible so just include simple brief headings to assist you.
Calculate the mean – in the first cell below Mean, E2, type **=average(B2:D2)** ; **Enter** or go to Formulas, More Functions, Statistical, select Average and then drag the mouse over the three cells.
Copy this formula to the other two cells and format the number to one decimal place – see page 19.
Now Copy and Paste these calculated values to your Word table.

Your table should now be as below.

Hydrogen peroxide concentration / %	Volume of oxygen collected / cm^3			
	Set 1	Set 2	Set 3	Mean
50	13	12	15	13.3
70	16	15	19	16.7
100	27	29	28	28.0

Go back to your spreadsheet. Select your three values for the hydrogen peroxide, hold down the ctrl key and select the three values for the mean. Click on Insert and select your graph, Scatter, and continue through the steps. See page 22.

- Remember to save your graph as a new sheet.

Go back to your Excel data table which is Sheet1 on the tabs at the bottom of the window..
You now need to calculate the difference between the mean and the maximum and minimum for each set of values.
Go to cell F2 and type **=max(B2:D2)-E2 ; Enter**. Copy the formula to the remaining cells.
Go to cell G2 and type **= E2-min(B2:D2) ; Enter**. Copy the formula to the remaining cells.
Copy and Paste this data into your Word table which should look as below.

HP conc	Set 1	Set 2	Set 3	Mean	Difference between mean and maximum	Difference between mean and minimum
50	13	12	15	13.3	1.7	1.3
70	16	15	19	16.7	2.3	1.7
100	27	29	28	28.0	1.0	1.0

Go back to Chart1.
On the ribbon select Chart Tools and Layout.
Click on Error Bars, then More Error Bar Options.
Error bars will appear on your graph but ignore this.
The Format Error Bars appears with the Vertical Error Bars by default. Also by default the Both circle, and the End Style Cap are checked. Most of the time these are what you want.

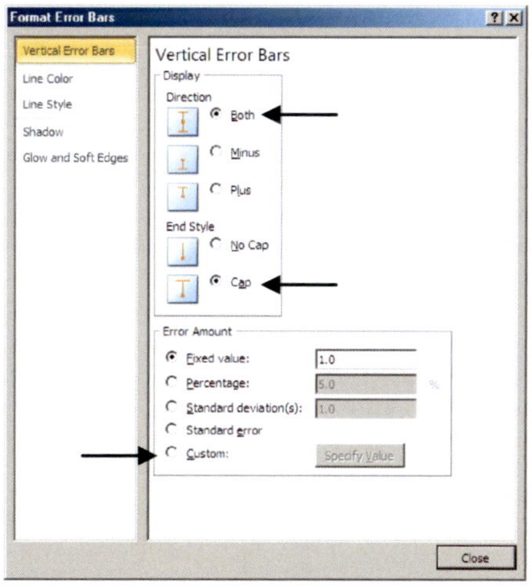

.

Select Custom, then Specify Value at the bottom of the Error Amount box. A new small box called Custom Error Bars appears with two windows – Positive Error Value and Negative Error Value.

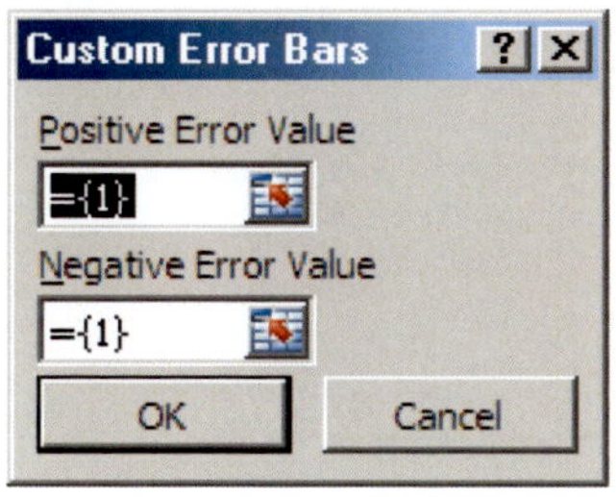

Click on Sheet1 at the bottom of your graph. Drag the mouse over the Difference between Mean and Maximum column and the references will appear in the Positive Error Value box.

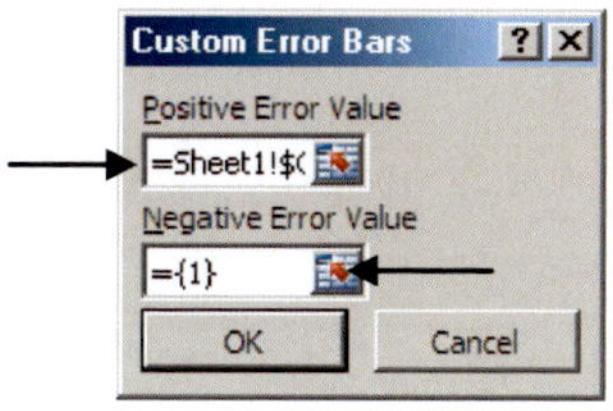

Click the red dot in the Negative Error Value box, again drag the mouse over the Difference between Mean and Minimum column in Sheet1 and click on the red dot.

The error bar references should now be in both Positive and Negative boxes in the Custom Error Bars box. Click OK and then close the Format Error Bars box.

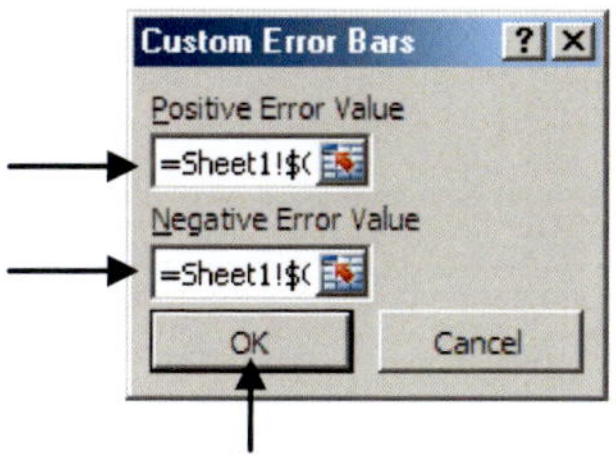

The Y error bars should now be on your graph but also oddly enough there are X (horizontal) error bars that Excel has decided to add for fun. If you don't want X error bars right click on any one and click Delete. However if you do, right click on any one and select Format Error Bars. The Horizontal Error Bars window appears. You can now follow the same procedure as before or choose a fixed value.

3. Uncertainty bars with different values

Look back at the data and graph on page 16. You may have decided that as the volume of gas increased so did the uncertainty, giving you the following data table.

temperature / ^{0}C	volume of gas collected / cm^3
5	26 ± 1
10	39 ± 2
15	46 ± 3
20	51 ± 4
25	57 ± 5

- On the Excel table you will need to put the uncertainly values in a separate column.

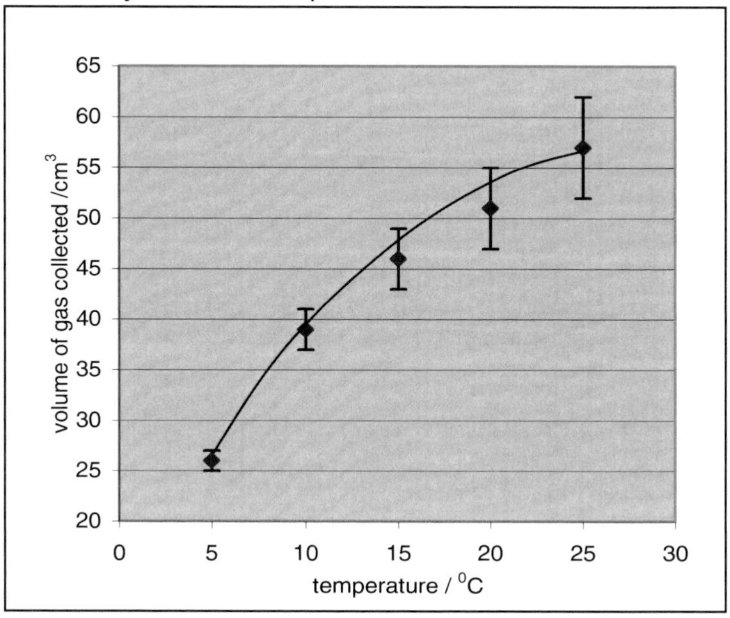

The procedure for adding the uncertainty bars is basically the same as for **Subsection 2** except that you select the column of uncertainty values for both the positive and negative values.

You would then add the line either by hand or using the curved line drawing tool in Word.

If you have 5 or more values for each data point then you may be able to calculate standard deviation.
Suppose you are investigating the effect of concentration of hydrogen peroxide on the release of oxygen by catalase and you have collected the data in the following table. This is the same as on page 25 for Sets 1-3 but I have now added Sets 4 and 5. For simplicity I have kept to only three values for the independent variable – in a real investigation you should have at least six.

Hydrogen peroxide concentration / %	Volume of oxygen collected / cm^3						
	Set 1	Set 2	Set 3	Set 4	Set 5	Mean	Standard deviation
50	13	12	15	14	11		
70	16	15	19	15	17		
100	27	29	28	27	25		

Copy and paste these on to your Excel spreadsheet as below. Remember that this is not going to be visible so there is no need to include all the detailed headings, though it is helpful to keep track of which column is which by putting in basic headings.

HP conc	Set 1	Set 2	Set 3	Set 4	Set 5	Mean	St Dev
50	13	12	15	14	11		
70	16	15	19	15	17		
100	27	29	28	27	25		

Calculate the mean and standard deviation – see page 19. Copy the formulas to the other two cells in each column and format the number to one decimal place.

HP conc	Set 1	Set 2	Set 3	Set 4	Set 5	Mean	St Dev
50	13	12	15	14	11	13.0	1.6
70	16	15	19	15	17	16.4	1.7
100	27	29	28	27	25	27.2	1.5

Now transfer these calculated values to your Word table.
Select all the mean values, right click and Copy, go back to your Word table and go to the top cell, right click and choose Overwrite Cells from the Paste Options. This will paste each mean into the correct cell. Repeat for standard deviation.
Your Word table should now be as below.

Hydrogen peroxide concentration / %	Volume of oxygen collected / cm^3						
	Set 1	Set 2	Set 3	Set 4	Set 5	Mean	Standard deviation
50	13	12	15	14	11	13.0	1.6
70	16	15	19	15	17	16.4	1.7
100	27	29	28	27	25	27.2	1.5

To select just the columns of data you want to plot select your values for the independent variable first (hydrogen peroxide in this case), hold down the ctrl key and select the values for the dependent variable (mean in this case). Click on Insert and select your graph, Scatter, and follow the procedure for plotting the graph – page 22 – and then the procedure for adding uncertainty bars – page 28.

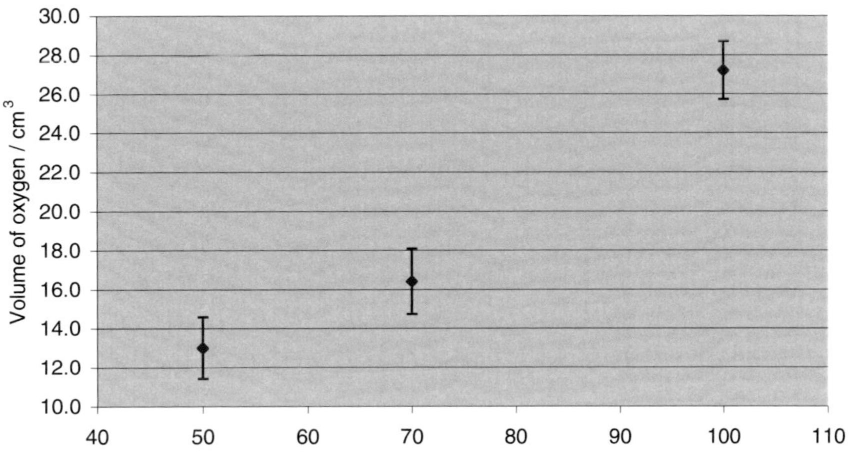

Graph 1. The volume of oxygen released with changing hydrogen peroxide concentration.

Completing the presentation

Once all the processing has been done save it to the desktop and then copy and paste it into your practical write-up in Word. You may need to re-size it. Now you can add the title and axis labels using text boxes (delete the line around the box).

In this example I let Excel draw the line, but can you see why this is wrong? What should I have done? The answer is on page 60.

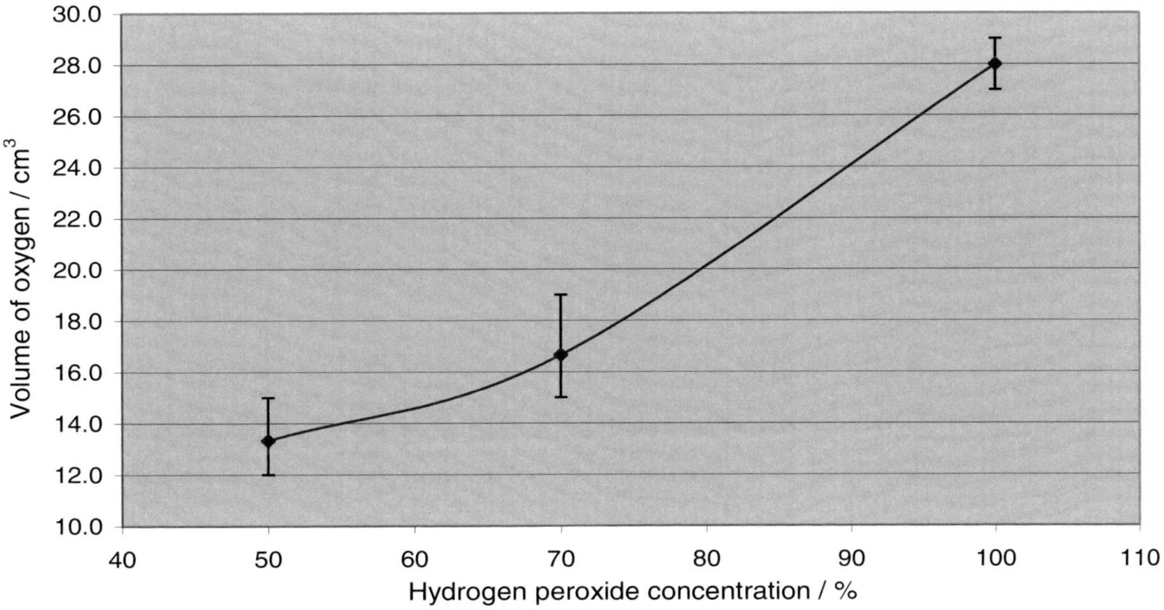

Graph 1. The volume of oxygen released with changing hydrogen peroxide concentration.

Scattergraphs and Correlation

This type of graph can be used to show if there is a relationship, or correlation, between the two sets of collected data. There are three categories – positive correlation, negative correlation, no correlation. These are illustrated below.

Important Just because the graph shows a correlation it does not mean that there is a causal relationship between the two variables. For example a plot of the number of people between 1960 and 1980 who chew gum against the number of people in the same period dying from lung cancer will show a positive correlation, but it does not necessarily mean that the increase in gum chewing is causing the increase in lung cancer or vice versa. Experimental data would need to be collected to provide evidence.

Data A	Data B
1	1
2	2
3	3
4	4
5	5
6	6
7	7

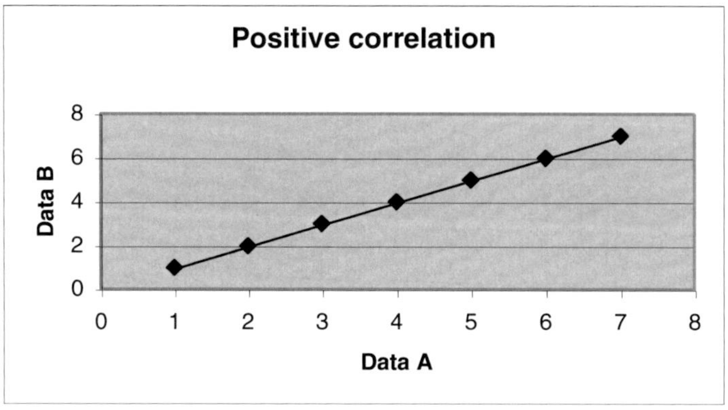

Data A	Data B
1	7
2	6
3	5
4	4
5	3
6	2
7	1

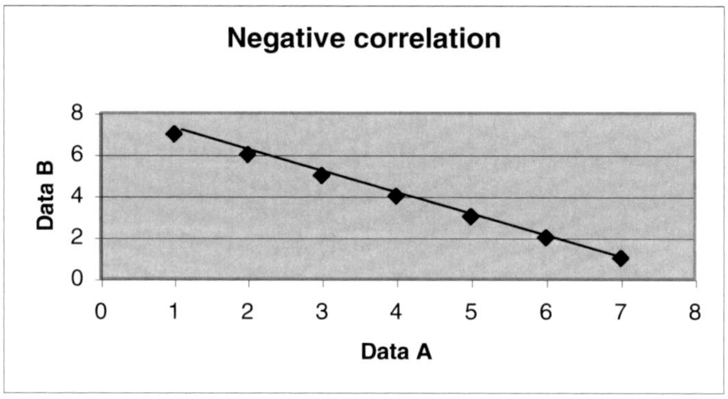

Data A	Data B
1	6
2	1
3	3
4	4
5	7
6	2
7	5

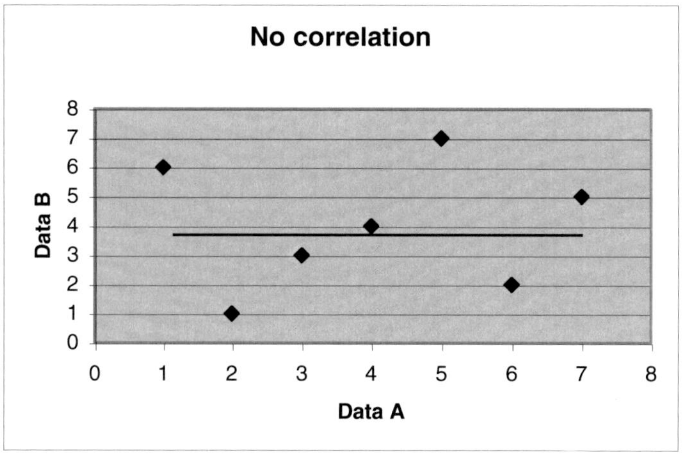

Column and Bar Graphs

Excel has a number of formats that you can play around with. There are no specific rules as to which format you use provided that it conveys clearly what you want. I suggest you avoid 3D ones – they don't improve interpretation and you cannot add uncertainty bars. Column / Bar graphs can also be compound in order to compare sets of data. Two examples are given below.

Example 1
A student had read about the experiments carried out by von Frisch on bees and wanted to investigate bee colour preferences. She set up clear glass dishes containing sugar water on different coloured backgrounds and counted the number of bees visiting each colour over a 2-hour period at midday.

Number of bees on each colour		
Red	Yellow	Blue
3	25	14

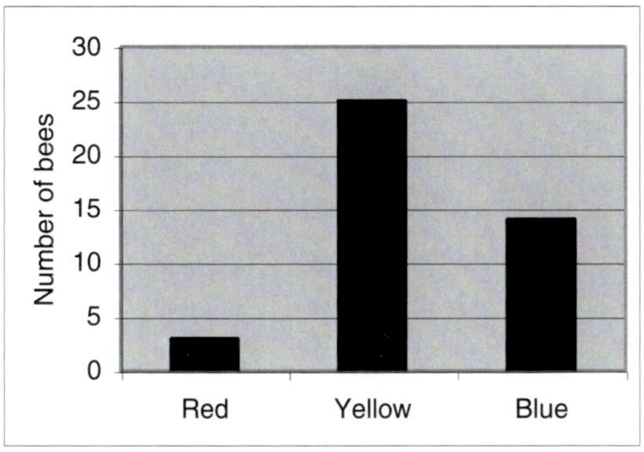

Graph 1. Number of bees on each colour in a two hour period.

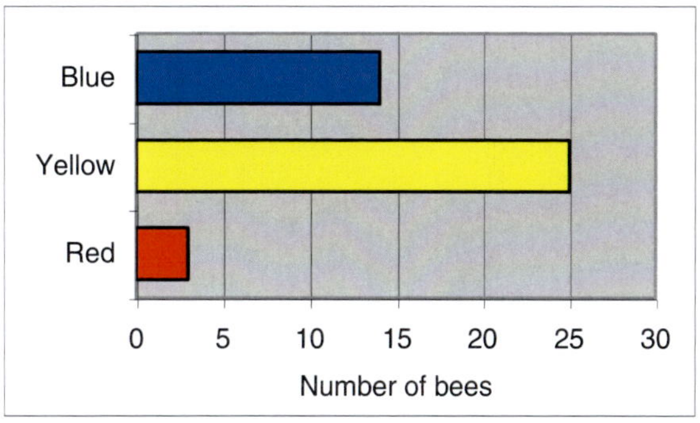

Graph 1. Number of bees on each colour in a two hour period.

Example 2
A student noticed that several species of plant growing in a shaded woodland had leaves a different shade of green from members of the same species growing in a meadow. He made acetone extracts of the chloroplast pigments and measured the % light transmission using a colorimeter.

Plant species	% light transmission ±3	
	Sun	Shade
A	45	61
B	36	40
C	22	59

Table 1. Colorimeter % transmission of acetone extracts from sun and shade leaves of three plant species.

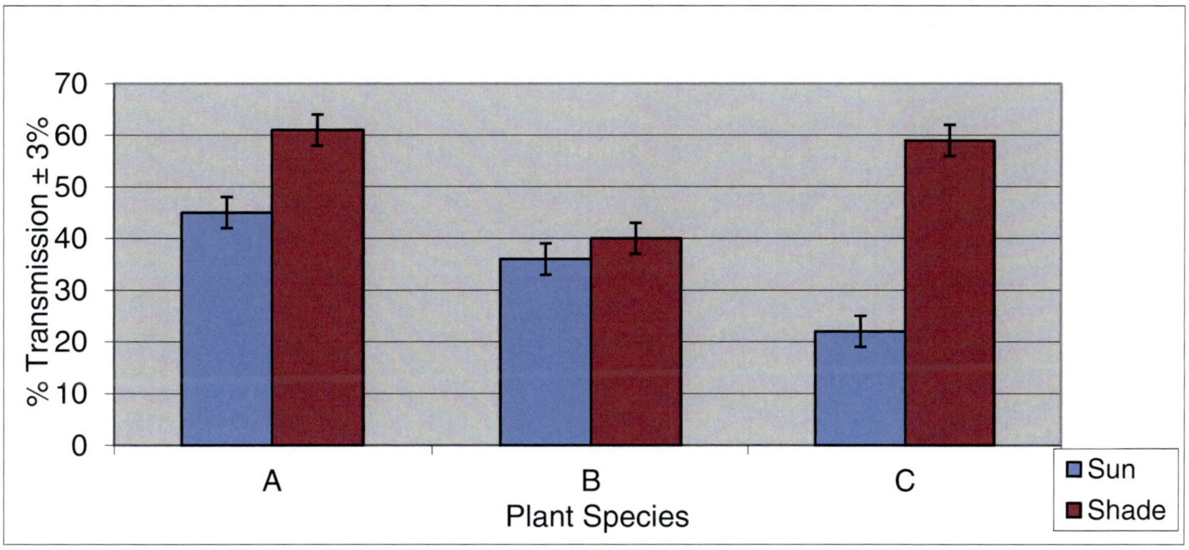

Graph 1. Colorimeter % transmission of acetone extracts from sun and shade leaves of three plant species.

Histograms

Once again Excel has a number of formats that you can use. However, it must always be a column graph. Select your data, select Insert, click Column and then the first of the 2-D ones.

Now the spaces between the columns need to be removed. Right click on any column, left click Format Data Series and move the Gap Width slider to zero.

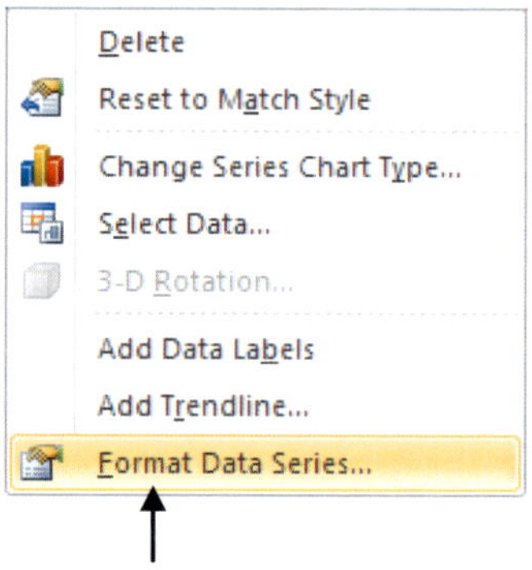

In the example below I have right clicked on the plot area and filled with a pale grey, and for the legend I've filled with white.

As usual add axis labels and title using text boxes without lines.

Histograms can also be compound in order to compare sets of data.

Example
A student collected the lengths of 24 leaves from each of two laurel bushes, one growing in a sunny environment and one in shade, and organised the data into groups as shown in the table below.

Leaf length / mm ±0.5	Number of leaves	
	sun	shade
90 – 94	2	1
95 – 99	3	1
100 – 104	3	2
105 – 109	5	4
110 – 114	4	7
115 – 119	3	7
120 – 124	3	5
125 – 129	1	3

Table 1. Grouped leaf length of sun and shade laurel leaves.

Here the sun leaves show a near normal distribution whereas the shade leaves show a positive skew.

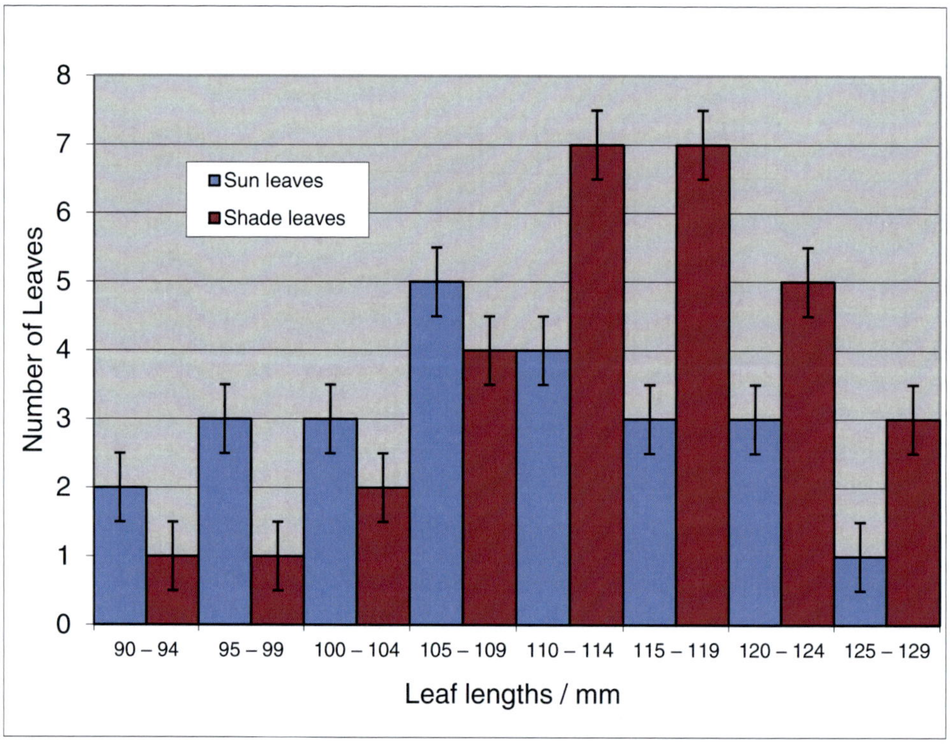

Graph 1. Grouped leaf length of sun and shade laurel leaves.

Pie Charts

Each segment of the pie represents a group, and may or may not be a percentage. The angle for each segment is calculated by –

$$d = \frac{V \times 360}{T}$$

where d = angle of segment,
V = actual value of the category,
T = grand total

Example.
The blood groups of two populations of 5000 people, one in England, and the second in Norway, were obtained. The data is shown below. (Note – this is not real data; it is made up for the example).

Blood group	England	Norway
A	1792	3110
B	850	1200
AB	209	343
O	2149	347
Total	*5000*	*5000*

Table 1. Numbers of people in England and Norway with different blood groups.

Once again there are rules for pie charts, and unfortunately Excel does not automatically follow these rules so you have to do a bit of data manipulation.
The rules are –

- Start at 12 o'clock and go clockwise.
- Arrange the segments of the first pie in order of decreasing size.
- In the second pie the order is the same as the first pie regardless of size of segment. This is so that it is easy to do a visual comparison.

Use a spreadsheet to do the calculations for you and then for the first data set sort into a descending order. For subsequent data sets you will have to move the data by hand so that the order of each group is the same as the first. Now you can insert the pie chart.

The formula in Excel is – =(cell ref *360)/total

Example

Blood group	England	Angle / degrees	Blood group	Norway	Angle / degrees
O	2149	155	O	347	25
A	1792	129	A	3110	86
B	850	61	B	1200	25
AB	209	15	AB	343	224
Total	*5000*	*360*	*Total*	*5000*	*360*

Table 1. Number of people in a sample of 5000 with the blood groups O, A, B and AB in England and Norway.

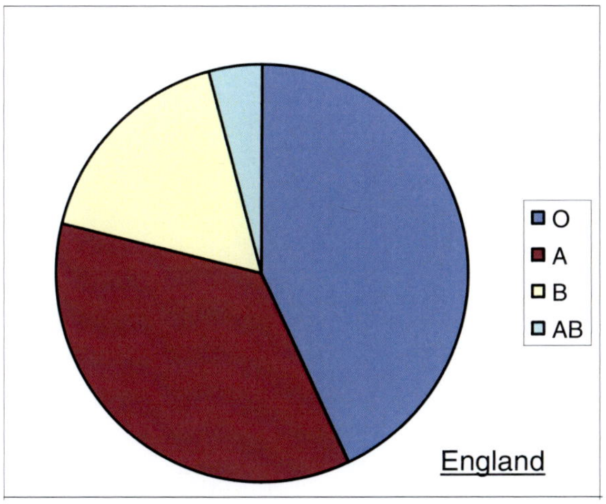

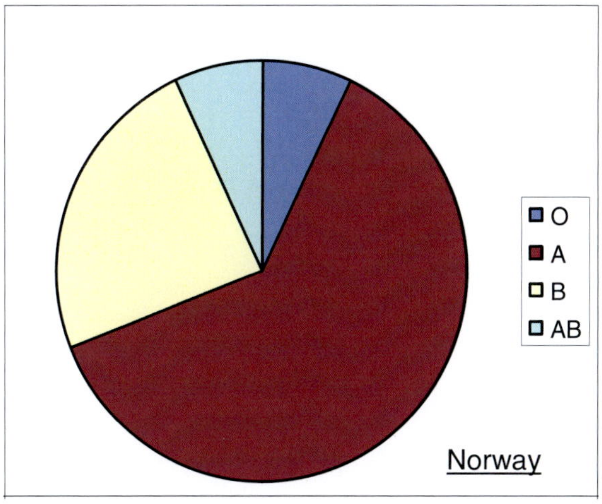

Graph 1. Number of people in a sample of 5000 with the blood groups O, A, B and AB in England and Norway.

Kite Diagrams

This is a method that allows you to quantify the distribution and abundance of one or more species of organism across a region, or regions.

- The data is usually collected by some form of sampling using either a line or a belt transect.
- Data for more than one organism can be collected, and as usual if comparisons are to be made the information must be presented together.

- You are effectively plotting a graph. The central axis can be either vertical or horizontal, but if you are recording from say, a wall or tree, it is logical to orientate it vertically so that it corresponds to the sample site.
- The points are plotted as mirror images off the central axis.
- Determine an appropriate scale. For example if your largest value is 10 organisms you can have a scale of 1 organism per cm and so plot 10cm on each side of the central axis. If though your largest value was 20 organisms your scale would have to be 2 organisms per cm as an A4 sheet of graph paper is only 28cm long.
- Having plotted all the points join them with ruled lines. In the example below I have shaded the diagrams but it is not necessary for you to do so as it takes too long to do it neatly.

Example
A student used a belt transect and quadrats to determine the distribution of green seaweeds and snails up a rocky shoreline. For both the snails and seaweed she used a 50cm quadrat. The snails were actual numbers, but for the seaweed she had to use an abundance scale.

Coverage Abundance Scale for Seaweed				
absent	1 – 25%	25 – 50%	50 – 75%	75 – 100%
0	1	2	3	4

Quadrat	Number of Snails	Abundance of Seaweed
1	18	0
2	18	0
3	20	1
4	10	1
5	5	3
6	3	2
7	0	4
8	1	5
9	0	5
10	0	4

Table 1. Number of snails and seaweed abundance, using the abundance scale above, in a 5m transect at St Margaret's bay, Dover. Quadrat 1 is closest to high water mark and quadrat 10 is at low water mark.

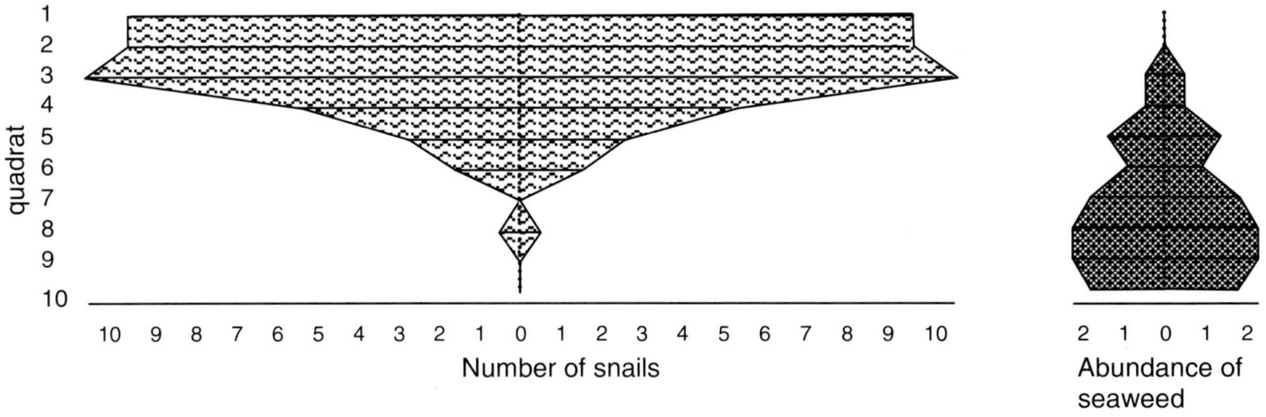

Graph 1. Kite Diagrams showing the Distribution of Snails and Seaweed in a 5m transect at St Margaret's bay, Dover. Quadrat 1 is closest to high water mark and quadrat 10 is at low water mark..

- ❖ Note how the two diagrams are aligned horizontally so that a direct comparison can be made on the distribution of the two organisms.
- ❖ Note also that there is no overlap between the two diagrams.

Excel does not do kite diagrams and they are difficult to draw in Word. The quickest and simplest way is to draw them by hand on graph paper.

Section 1.3

Conclusion and Evaluation

Conclusion and Evaluation	Drawing conclusions	Evaluating procedure(s) and results	Improving the investigation
Complete	Gives a valid conclusion based on the correct interpretation of the results, with an explanation, and, where appropriate, compares results with literature values.	Evaluates procedure(s) and results including limitations, weaknesses or errors.	Identifies weaknesses and states realistic suggestions to improve the investigation.

Conclusion and Evaluation needs 4 sub-headings.

- **Conclusion**
- **Explanation of Conclusion**
- **Evaluation of Results**
- **Evaluation of the Procedure**

Note that these sub-headings do not mimic the Assessment strands. This is because these are simply what the examiner is assessing.
The first and second sub-headings are the first strand;
The third sub-heading is from the second strand;
The fourth sub-heading is from both the second and third strands.

Conclusion

- This needs to be a clear, simple and precise statement.
- There may be more than one conclusion.

Poor example : *There is a difference in the number of attacks by the holly leaf miner and the height in the hedge.*

Good example : *There is a significantly greater number of attacks by the holly leaf miner (Phytomyza ilicis) above a height of 1000mm in the holly hedge (Ilex* sp.) *compared to below 1000mm.*

Explanation of Conclusion

Here you are giving reasons as to why you obtained the results you did. The level of explanation should be appropriate to SL or HL.

- Refer to your data and your processing of the data, ie. how your graph(s) and statistical analysis support your conclusion.
- Add further support with a scientific explanation from your lessons, text books or web sites. Remember that you MUST make correct reference to book or web sources – see the box below.
- If you suggested a hypothesis in Design is it supported? Refer to your scientific explanation.

Referencing

The neatest way to do this is to use footnotes. When you quote something from a book or other source, or you refer to something from a book, then follow it with a number suffix. Then in the footer give this number and a brief reference to the source quoted, including the page number if relevant. The full details of the source are then given in a bibliography at the end of your report. See page 6.

Example –

'Since the graph of enzyme activity drops after 50°C I think that the enzyme has been denatured. "When an enzyme is denatured, the cross-links are broken and the polypeptide chains open up and become randomly arranged" [2]. This means the active site has lost its shape.'

[2] Roberts, Reiss and Monger p127

Evaluation of the Results

- Look critically at your data, including the graphs.
- How reliable is it? See the next page about this word 'reliable'.
    - Do the repeats support each other?
    - Are any uncertainties large enough to have a significant effect?
    - How could such uncertainties have arisen?
    - How large is the standard deviation? See page 19.
    - Can you draw a good line of best fit on the graph or could there be alternative lines of best fit? See page 17 for an example. A second example is shown below.
    - Does the graph match your hypothesis (if you put one forward) either entirely or at least in part?
    - If you have done a statistical analysis such as a t-test or Mann-Whitney U test (See the Statistics section on pages 41 to 46) then you will have calculated a value that you compared with the critical value for the particular test. If the calculated value is close to the critical value then this means your conclusion is less reliable – see page 37. The type of statistical test you have used is also relevant – the t-test is a more powerful test than the Mann-Whitney U test.

Important point

You should aim to write a comment about as many of these points as you can. Each time explain your comment.

Here is a simple example concerning the turning behaviour of woodlice.

Temperature / ^{0}C	Activity / Number of turns 5 minutes^{-1}								
	Trial 1	Trial 2	Trial 3	Trial 4	Trial 5	Mean	St Dev	Corrected Mean	Corrected SD
15	78	81	77	80	79	79	1.58	79	1.58
18	79	115	84	82	79	88	15.35	81	3.54
25	110	114	112	113	112	112	1.48	112	1.48
30	152	139	147	141	153	146	6.31	146	6.31
35	115	124	118	119	122	120	3.51	120	3.51

Table 1. Number of turns per 5 minutes made by woodlice at different temperatures, showing both raw and processed data.

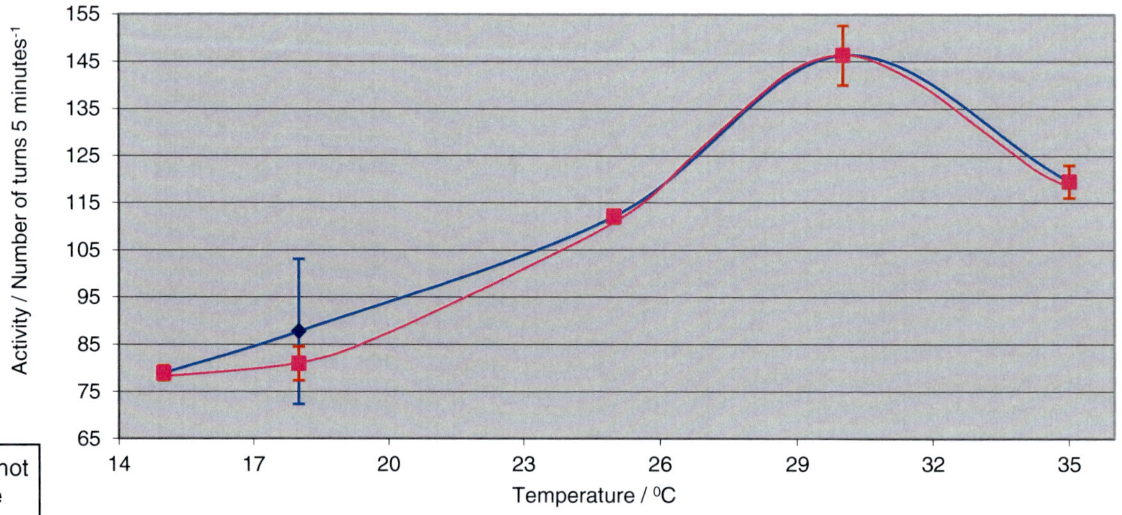

For simplicity I have not included temperature uncertainty bars.

Graph 1. Number of turns made by woodlice during 5 minutes at different temperatures.

The value for trial 2 at 18°C is very different from the other 4 trials. If we include it in the mean calculation it appears to give a mean that fits the pattern of the means for temperatures 15 – 30°C. However look at the standard deviation. It is particularly large. If we exclude it from the calculation the corrected mean and corrected standard deviation look much better. Now look at the graph. The blue line shows the uncorrected mean values and again it looks reasonable. The pink line though shows the corrected values and we might consider this to be a better line. This one value though is still within +2 standard deviations of the mean and therefore we should not consider it as an anomaly.

The standard deviation for 30°C is a little higher than the others because the values range from 139 to 153. However we can still consider this range to be small because the standard deviation is well below 33% of the mean.

I have added the standard deviation bars using the same colours as the lines and you can see that the pink line falls well within the blue standard deviation at 18°C but the blue line does not fall within the pink standard deviation. I therefore feel that the corrected data is a better representation of the turning behaviour of the woodlice.

Notice though that being able to calculate standard deviation allows a much more detailed analysis of your data, and hence the value of collecting enough data to be able to calculate this. Remember though that 5 values really is pushing the boundary for calculating standard deviation and it would be much better to have more if possible.

Evaluation of the Procedure

Important point

NEVER make statements such as "I could have read the thermometer more accurately" or "I might have measured the volume incorrectly". This simply indicates to your teacher, and the moderator, that you are rather incompetent and so you cannot possibly get full marks for Manipulative Skills!

'**Accurate**' and '**Reliable**' are two important words to use.

- Accuracy is in the correct and careful use of the best apparatus available to you and taking measurements carefully.
- Reliability is in having enough data to be able to process it fully, including perhaps a statistical analysis, and then draw firm conclusions.

- ➢ Aim to identify at least three clear weaknesses and provide a realistic improvement for each.
- ➢ It would though be advisable to have more than three in case the examiner does not accept some of them.
- ➢ **It is better to identify the weakness and suggest the improvement before going on to the next weakness.**
- ➢ Remember that the improvement could be something that you did while you were carrying out the investigation regardless of whether you planned it or you were following instructions given to you by your teacher.
- ➢ The improvement must not be superficial. For example 'I should take more readings' is clearly too simplistic and rather indicates you planned it badly in the first place!

What is it that you are evaluating? It could be an investigation that you have planned or it could be one where your teacher has given you a set of instructions to follow.

Ideally if you have planned it then you will have done everything possible to make it accurate and reliable of course! However you may have been limited by the apparatus available to you, so improvements could be using better equipment such as –

- o a digital thermometer;
- o data loggers;
- o buffer solutions to control pH;
- o a colorimeter to measure light transmission;
- o more precise equipment such as syringes or a micropipette to measure very small volumes;
- o a thermostatic water bath to control temperature;
- o a fluorescent lamp to prevent the heating effect of a filament lamp;
- o coloured filters that are more precise about the wavelength of light they allow through.

Alternatively aspects of the method might be improved such as –

- o taking measurements at intermediate values of the independent variable to improve the accuracy of the graph – with reasoning;
- o A greater range for the independent variable – with reasoning.

Section 1.4

Choosing the Right Statistics

This can be a bit of a nightmare, but luckily there is a simple key on the next page to help you select the right one.

Levels of Data

Data can be collected at three different levels.

- Interval data is of high quality because it involves processing the actual measurements involved, so a powerful, and therefore reliable, analysis can be done.
- Ordinal data is good quality but only tells us about the order of a set of data, so its value is limited.
- Categorical data is simple data and involves counting the frequency of something. In terms of statistical analysis it is poor quality.

Interval data has numbers arranged on a scale, with equal units between each measurement.	**Ordinal data** is ranked in a series from lowest to highest, but the distances between each measurement may not be the same.	**Categorical data** can be divided into clear categories.

Interval Data

Interval level data is the most usual form of data that you will collect in your investigations. These are true measurements such as volumes, distances, times. Most of the statistics tests use interval level data, but sometimes the data you have collected is insufficient to allow you to use one of these tests. Therefore for statistical analysis you need to treat the data at the ordinal level. This will be explained later.

Ordinal Data

With these measurements you can say that one is bigger or smaller than another but you can only arrange the data in an order – it does not tell us anything about the distance between the measurements. For example we can say that one tree has some lichen on it, another has more and a third tree even more, so we can put them in the order 1, 2 and 3, but we cannot say that tree 2 has twice as much lichen on it than tree 1.

Categorical Data

Here we simply put the data into categories, so it belongs to this or that category. The categories cannot be arranged in any order. Examples would be human eye colours or skin colours, coloured flowers/white flowers, long fur/short fur, smokers/non-smokers, long wings/short wings. The number of categories should be few or analysis becomes tedious. Aim for not more than four.

Types of Measurement

Unmatched or Independent measurements

Two or more sets of data have been collected from different organisms or parts of organisms, eg pulse rates of 20 students aged 11 years and 20 students aged 18 years, or the lengths of 20 leaves on the sunny side of a hedge and 20 leaves on the shaded side.

Matched or Paired measurements

Sometimes two measurements are in pairs. For example, measuring the size and temperature of an anthill – a particular temperature must be matched with a particular anthill.

Repeated measurements

Two or more sets of data have been collected from one organism with changing conditions, eg pulse rate of a student before and after taking caffeine. It is though possible to collate data from several different organisms for the analysis, though each organism must have participated in each condition.

Statistics Route Planner

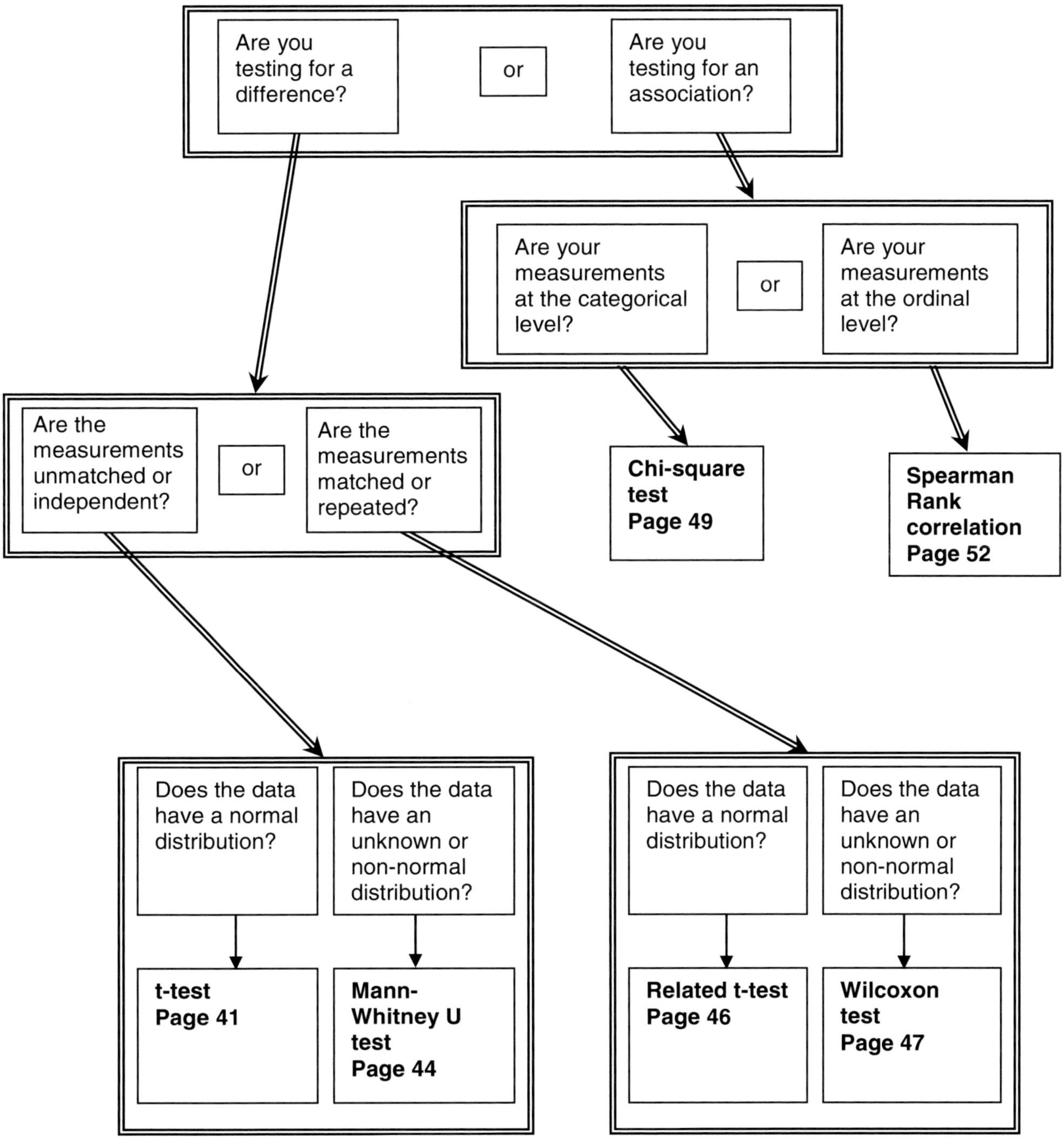

There are many other statistical tests but these six are the commonly used ones.
If you want to go further then very useful statistics books are –

The OU Project Guide. *Fieldwork and Statistics for Ecological Projects*. Neil Chalmers, Phil Parker, Kevin McConway. Field Studies Council.
Advanced Biology : Statistics. Andrew Edmondson and David Druce. Oxford University Press. 1996.
J.W.Garvin. *Skills in Advanced Biology Vol 1 – Dealing with Data*. Stanley Thornes (Publishers) Ltd 1992

The Hypothesis and Significance Testing

A hypothesis is a prediction of the outcome of the investigation. There are two forms that the hypothesis can take and these are in opposition to each other. The statistical test you choose aims to prove one hypothesis correct and the other one wrong.
The two forms of the hypothesis are the Null Hypothesis, called H_0, and the Alternative Hypothesis, called H_1.

The Null Hypothesis, H_0 and the Alternative Hypothesis, H_1

The null hypothesis is in effect a negative hypothesis because it is stating that there is no link between the sets of data, whereas the alternative hypothesis states that there is. But why do we need both types of hypothesis? Look at these examples.

Example 1. A new selective weedkiller is being tried out on a field. Half the field is sprayed with the weedkiller and the other half sprayed with water as the control. We could put forward both types of hypothesis.
The null hypothesis states that *'There is no difference in the weed population in the two halves of the field after treatment'.*
The alternative hypothesis states that *'The weedkiller decreases the number of weeds in the half of the field where it is used'.*

Example 2. Ivy growing in the shade will have less light available for photosynthesis whereas one growing on a sunny wall will have plenty of light. The leaves are likely to be different in size.
The null hypothesis would state that *'There is no difference in the surface area of the leaves of the shaded plant and leaves of the sunny plant'.*
The alternative hypothesis states that *'The surface area of the leaves of the shaded plant is greater than the surface area of the leaves of the sunny plant".*

The significance test then confirms which hypothesis to accept and which to reject. If the null hypothesis is accepted then there is no difference between the samples; if rejected then there is and we may be able to accept the alternative hypothesis.
However we need to be careful about which form of the test we use as there are two different types that can be performed, either a **one-tailed** or a **two-tailed** test. Most of the time we use the two-tailed test but sometimes a better result can be obtained with a one-tailed test – see page 59.

Example 3. A student investigated colour vision in bees by putting sugar water in glass dishes above different coloured paper to see if they preferred yellow to blue. Here we have no idea which colour the bees would choose – it would be pure guesswork and so we cannot state an alternative hypothesis.
The null hypothesis states that '*Bees have no preference for yellow or blue*'.
If we then prove the null hypothesis to be wrong we know that the bees do prefer one colour over the other and the numbers will tell us which is the preferred colour.

Significance Level, Probability, and the Critical Value

For the t-test (both types), the Wilcoxon Matched Pairs test, and the Chi Squared test, the critical value in Biology is usually taken at a significance level of 5% which is the same as a probability of 0.05. Thus the critical values are those in the column under 5% or 0.05.

- If your significance level or probability is less than 5% or 0.05 then there is a significant difference between your sets of data. This is because the probability of a difference occurring by chance is 5 times (or less) in 100, or put the other way, 95 times in 100 the difference is caused by some factor.

The other statistical tests also have critical values. If the number that you have calculated is close to the critical value then that will affect, one way or the other, the reliability of your conclusion.

<u>Example 1</u>. If the value you calculated for t in a t-test was 2.05 for 38 degrees of freedom, critical value 2.02, then your conclusion that there is a significant difference between the data sets must be exceedingly cautious. However if the calculated t value was 2.44 then you can be much more confident in the difference, (probability 0.02), and very confident if the calculated t value was 2.77, (probability 0.01).

<u>Example 2.</u> If the value you calculated in a Spearman Rank Correlation test was 0.73 and the critical value was 0.74 then that indicates a negative correlation because it is less than the critical value. However it is so close to the critical value your conclusion is not reliable. On the other hand if your calculated value was 0.52 then that indicates a strong negative correlation and your conclusion is much more reliable.

Section 1.4.1

Putting Statistics into Practice

Testing for a Difference

Unmatched or Independent Measurements

❖ t-test

This test is the one to use if the data –

- Is unmatched;
- Is at the interval level;
- Has a minimum sample size of 15 for each data set;
- Has a normal distribution.

It is a powerful test in that it can distinguish small differences between the sets of data, though the smaller the sample size the larger the difference between the means has to be to be detected. There does not need to be the same number of values in each data set. While collecting the data, or after collection, you will need to check the distribution because it <u>must</u> be normal, or very near normal, for the test to work.. Use the frequency tally system given earlier.

Example

A student noticed that there appeared to be a difference in the density of vegetation growing at ground level in a deciduous wood and a coniferous wood. Knowing that light was a limiting factor he measured light intensity at 15 randomly selected points within the two woods. He checked that the data formed a normal distribution by carrying out a frequency tally. Both sets were normal, and each value was unrelated, so he could then do a t-test.
His null hypothesis was –

There is no significant difference between the light intensities in the two woods.

If the raw data is sorted in the table it is easy to produce classes and a frequency tally to check distribution.

Deciduous wood					
Site n	Light intensity / arbitrary units x_1	Sorted light intensity / arbitrary units	Class	Frequency	x_1^2
1	10.5	9.6	9.5 - 9.9	|	110.25
2	9.6	10.1	10.0 -10.4	||	92.16
3	10.1	10.4	10.5 -10.9	||||	102.01
4	11.6	10.5	11.0 -11.4	||||	etc
5	11.6	10.5	11.5 -11.9	|||	
6	11.3	10.6	12.0 -12.4	|	
7	10.6	10.7			
8	10.4	11.0			
9	12.4	11.1			
10	11.3	11.3			
11	10.7	11.3			
12	10.5	11.5			
13	11.5	11.6			
14	11.1	11.6			
15	11.0	12.4			
$\sum x_1$	164.2			$\sum x_1^2$	1804.40

Note the use of the decimal tab to align the decimal points.

<u>Table 1. Raw and sorted data for light intensity in the deciduous wood.</u>

Repeat this with the coniferous data.

<table>
<tr><th colspan="6">Coniferous wood</th></tr>
<tr><th>Site
n</th><th>Light intensity / arbitrary units
x_1</th><th>Sorted light intensity / arbitrary units</th><th>Class</th><th>Frequency</th><th>x_1^2</th></tr>
<tr><td>1</td><td>9.1</td><td>9.1</td><td>9.0 - 9.4</td><td>||</td><td>82.81</td></tr>
<tr><td>2</td><td>10.3</td><td>9.3</td><td>9.5 - 9.9</td><td>||||</td><td>106.09</td></tr>
<tr><td>3</td><td>10.8</td><td>9.6</td><td>10.0 -10.4</td><td>|||||</td><td>116.64</td></tr>
<tr><td>4</td><td>10.3</td><td>9.7</td><td>10.5 -10.9</td><td>|||</td><td>etc</td></tr>
<tr><td>5</td><td>9.6</td><td>9.7</td><td>11.0 -11.4</td><td>|</td><td></td></tr>
<tr><td>6</td><td>11.1</td><td>9.9</td><td></td><td></td><td></td></tr>
<tr><td>7</td><td>9.3</td><td>10.2</td><td></td><td></td><td></td></tr>
<tr><td>8</td><td>10.5</td><td>10.2</td><td></td><td></td><td></td></tr>
<tr><td>9</td><td>10.4</td><td>10.3</td><td></td><td></td><td></td></tr>
<tr><td>10</td><td>9.7</td><td>10.3</td><td></td><td></td><td></td></tr>
<tr><td>11</td><td>10.2</td><td>10.4</td><td></td><td></td><td></td></tr>
<tr><td>12</td><td>10.2</td><td>10.5</td><td></td><td></td><td></td></tr>
<tr><td>13</td><td>9.7</td><td>10.8</td><td></td><td></td><td></td></tr>
<tr><td>14</td><td>10.9</td><td>10.9</td><td></td><td></td><td></td></tr>
<tr><td>15</td><td>9.9</td><td>11.1</td><td></td><td></td><td></td></tr>
<tr><td>$\sum x_2$</td><td>152.0</td><td></td><td></td><td>$\sum x_2^2$</td><td>1544.98</td></tr>
</table>

Table 2. Raw and sorted data for light intensity in the coniferous wood.

Calculate the means and variances for both sets of data. Remember that the variance is the square of the standard deviation – see the formulae on page 54.

Excel has a function for the t-test but it does not return a value for t. Instead it calculates the probability, p. If this value is less than 0.05 this is the same as 5%, ie there is a statistically significant difference between the two sets of data.

$$\bar{x}_1 = \frac{164.2}{15} = 10.95 \qquad \text{Variance 1} \quad s_1^2 = \frac{\sum (x-\bar{x})^2}{n-1} = 0.50$$

$$\bar{x}_2 = \frac{152.0}{15} = 10.13 \qquad \text{Variance 2} \quad s_2^2 = \frac{\sum (x-\bar{x})^2}{n-1} = 0.34$$

Site	Light intensity / arbitrary units	
	Deciduous Wood	Coniferous Wood
1	10.5	9.1
2	9.6	10.3
3	10.1	10.8
4	11.6	10.3
5	11.6	9.6
6	11.3	11.1
7	10.6	9.3
8	10.4	10.5
9	12.4	10.4
10	11.3	9.7
11	10.7	10.2
12	10.5	10.2
13	11.5	9.7
14	11.1	10.9
15	11.0	9.9
Mean	10.95	10.13
Variance	0.50	0.34
	t-test probability	0.002

Table 3. Calculations of the mean, variance and t-test probability.

To use Excel to calculate the mean and variance follow these instructions.

Copy and paste the two sets of data into a spreadsheet.
Place cursor in cell below the first set of data.
Click on Formulas and then More Functions;
Select Statistical;
Select Average;
Select the required cells;
Click OK;
Repeat for second set of data.

Place cursor in cell below the mean.
Click on Formulas and then More Functions;
Select Statistical;
Select Var.S;
Select the required cells;
Click OK;
Repeat for second set of data.

To use Excel to calculate probability for the t-test follow these instructions.

Place cursor in an empty cell.
Click on Formulas and then More Functions;
Select Statistical;
Select T.Test;

Click OK;
You now have four boxes to complete and the cursor is flashing in the first box, Array1.
Select the first set of values in your data table. As you do this the cell references appear in Array1.
Click in Array 2. Select the second set of values in your data table
Click in the third box, Tails, and type 1 or 2.*
Click in the last box, Type, and type 1 if the data is matched or paired, (see page 39) or 3. Always assume the variances are unequal.
In our example this returns a probability of 0.002 to 3dp.

*See page 59 for information on one and two-tailed tests.

The formula for t is -

$$t = \frac{|\bar{x}_1 - \bar{x}_2|}{\sqrt{\frac{s_1^2}{n_1} + \frac{s_2^2}{n_2}}}$$

The vertical lines on each side of the $\bar{x}_1 - \bar{x}_2$ indicate that the difference is always treated as a positive value even if it is negative. This is because choosing which is set 1 and which is set 2 is random.

$$t = \frac{|10.95 - 10.13|}{\sqrt{\frac{0.50}{15} + \frac{0.34}{15}}}$$

$t = 3.42$

The degrees of freedom (df) for the t-test are calculated by $(n_1 + n_2) - 2$. In this case both sample sizes are 15 so df = 15 + 15 – 2 = 28. We look this up on the t table (page 54) and find that the t value of 3.42 for 28 degrees of freedom is less than 1%. This means that the difference between the two sets of data is highly significant and we can reject the null hypothesis.

If we have used Excel to calculate the probability we have a figure of 0.002 using the two-tailed test. (We can only use the two-tailed test because we cannot really be sure which woodland has the lower and which the higher light intensity.) This is much less than the probability of 0.05 which is the level of significance. This means that the difference between the two sets of data is highly significant and we can reject the null hypothesis.

Summary

- Degrees of freedom = (sample 1 + sample 2) – 2
- 5% is the significance level or a probability of 0.05.
- If the calculated value of t is less than the critical value or the probability is greater than 0.05 then there is no significant difference between the sets of data.
- The null hypothesis H_0 can be accepted.
- If the calculated value is greater than the critical value or the probability is less than 0.05 then there is a significant difference between the sets of data.
- The alternative hypothesis H_1 can be accepted.

❖ Mann-Whitney U test

This test is the one to use if the data –

- Is unmatched;
- Is at the ordinal level;
- Is at the interval level but the distribution is not normal;
- Has a minimum of 7 values for each data set.

It is based on placing the data in rank order, the smallest being the lowest rank and the largest the highest rank. As with the t-test the number of values in each data set does not have to be the same.

Example

A student collected banded snails from under two different hedges using 30cm quadrats. The raw and sorted data is shown in the tables below.
Her null hypothesis was–

There is no difference in the number of banded snails in the two hedges.

	Number of banded snails in each 30cm quadrat	
Quadrat	Hedge 1	Hedge 2
1	0	12
2	3	5
3	6	19
4	4	18
5	1	12
6	3	14
7	0	20

Hedge 1	Number of banded snails in each 30cm quadrat			
Quadrat	Raw	Sorted	Class	Frequency
1	0	0	0	| |
2	3	0	1	|
3	6	1	3	| |
4	4	3	4	|
5	1	3	6	|
6	3	4		
7	0	6		

Hedge 2	Number of banded snails in each 30cm quadrat			
Quadrat	Raw	Sorted	Class	Frequency
1	12	5	5	|
2	5	12	12	| |
3	19	12	14	|
4	18	14	18	|
5	12	18	19	|
6	14	19	20	|
7	20	20		

Tables to show the raw and sorted data for numbers of snails collected using 30cm quadrats in two hedges.

The number of values is small and the data does not form a normal distribution so we cannot use the t-test. We therefore have to use a test that is not so powerful, ie we cannot be quite so sure of the result. The sorted data in fact forms a rank order, so we rearrange the table as below.

Hedge	Data arranged in increasing order							Median
1	0	0	1	3	3	4	6	3
2	5	12	12	14	18	19	20	14

We now need to form another table showing the ranking from 1 upwards. Numbers of equal value are given the same rank.

The first two values for hedge 1 are 0, and they form ranks 1 and 2. Since they must have the same rank they are given the mean of ranks 1 and 2, ie. 1.5.
The values for the two hedges overlap, and the ranking must follow the order of the values. Thus the value of 5 in hedge 2 must have the rank position between the values of 4 and 6 for hedge 1.

Hedge 1	**0**	**0**	**1**	**3**	**3**	**4**		**6**							
Rank R_1	1.5	1.5	3	4.5	4.5	6		8							$\sum R_1 = 29$
Rank R_2							7		9.5	9.5	11	12	13	14	$\sum R_2 = 76$
Hedge 2							**5**		**12**	**12**	**14**	**18**	**19**	**20**	

The ranks are then summed for each hedge. The statistic we are using is called the Mann-Whitney U test, so the next step is to find the U value for each hedge.
The formula is –
For hedge 1 $U_1 = n_1 \times n_2 + \frac{1}{2} n_1 (n_1 + 1) - \sum R_1$
For hedge 2 $U_2 = n_1 \times n_2 + \frac{1}{2} n_2 (n_2 + 1) - \sum R_2$

Where n_1 is the number of samples in hedge 1, and n_2 is the number of samples in hedge 2.
Thus $U_1 = 48$
$U_2 = 1$.

Using the values of n as co-ordinates we find the critical value for U in the table. The complete table is on page 55.

		Values of n_1						
		1	2	3	4	5	6	7
Values of n_2	1							
	2							
	3					0	1	1
	4				0	1	2	3
	5			0	1	2	3	5
	6			1	2	3	5	6
	7			1	3	5	6	8

We compare the smallest of our U values with this, and if it is equal to or less than the critical value then there is a significant difference between the two sets of data. The U value from the table is 8, and our smallest U value is 1, which is less than 8. Thus there is a significant difference between the data from the two hedges, and the student can reject her null hypothesis.

Summary

- The critical value is found by using the number of samples in each data set as co-ordinates.
- Compare the smallest value of U with the critical value.
- If the smallest value of U is greater than the critical value then there is no significant difference between the two sets of data.
- The null hypothesis H_0 can be accepted.
- If the smallest value of U is equal to or less than the critical value then there is a significant difference between the two sets of data.
- The alternative hypothesis H_1 can be accepted.

Testing for a Difference

Matched, Paired or Repeated Measurements

❖ Related t-test

This test is the one to use if the data –

- Is matched, paired or repeated,
- Is at the interval level,
- Has a minimum sample size of 15 for each data set,
- Has a normal distribution.

> If you are using Excel then for Type you enter 1.

The basic principles of this test are the same as for the t-test, but the two sets of values are related in that they are done on the same organism, or that they are matched pairs.

The formula is –

$$t = \frac{\bar{d}}{\sqrt{\dfrac{\sum d^2 - (\sum d)^2 / n}{n(n-1)}}}$$

Where
d = the difference between the pairs of values, and
n = the number of values.

degrees of freedom = n - 1

Example

A student wanted to investigate the effect of noise on concentration. He chose 15 students and carried out the test in silent conditions. He then repeated the test but at the same time played a tape recording of a noisy party. His null hypothesis was – *There will be no difference in the test results taken under silent or noisy conditions.*

Student	Score in situation A Quiet	Score in situation B Noisy	Difference between score A and score B d	Difference Sorted	Tally	d^2
1	20	17	3	-1	|	9
2	18	17	1	0		1
3	9	7	2	0	||	4
4	14	14	0	1		0
5	14	12	2	1	||	4
6	17	9	8	2		64
7	10	8	2	2		4
8	9	8	1	2		1
9	15	11	4	2	||||	16
10	7	4	3	3		9
11	15	13	2	3		4
12	12	13	-1	3	|||	1
13	8	8	0	4	|	0
14	17	14	3	5	|	9
15	20	15	5	8	|	5
			$\sum d = 35$			$\sum d^2 = 131$

Table 1. Raw and processed data for test scores in quiet and noisy conditions.

From the tally chart of the differences it can be seen that the distribution is nearly normal, and therefore we can use the related t-test.

$$t = \frac{2.33}{\sqrt{\dfrac{151-(15)^2/15}{15(15-1)}}} \qquad t = \frac{2.33}{\sqrt{\dfrac{151-81.7}{210}}} \qquad t = \frac{2.33}{\sqrt{0.33}}$$

t = 4.09

df = n – 1 = 15 – 1 = 14

We use the same table of t distribution as for the t-test, (page 54), and looking up under df = 14 we find that our value of 4.09 is below the significance value for 1% This means that the difference is highly significant and we can reject the null hypothesis. The test results <u>were</u> significantly worse when done under noisy conditions.

❖ Wilcoxon test

This test is the one to use if the data –

- Is matched,
- Is at the interval level,
- Has symmetrical distributions,
- Has between 5 and 15 non-zero differences between matched measurements,
- Does not have a normal distribution.

Since it is a weaker test than the Related t-test we cannot be quite so sure of the significance of the result.

Example

A student had noticed that there seemed to be more moss growing on one side of the trees in a woodland than there was on the opposite side. She selected 12 trees randomly and measured the area of trunk covered by moss from ground level up to 1m. The data is shown in the table below. Her null hypothesis was – *There is no difference between the area of moss on the north and south sides of the trees.*

Tree	Area of moss on north side / cm^2	Area of moss on south side / cm^2	Difference between north and south sides
1	44	36	+8
2	44	39	+5
3	45	39	+6
4	47	43	+4
5	48	49	-1
6	52	49	+3
7	57	51	+6
8	52	54	-2
9	52	58	-6
10	57	60	-3
11	62	62	0
12	67	72	-5

Table 1. Raw and partly processed data for moss areas on north and south sides of trees.

The next step is to produce a rank order of these differences, but ignoring both the minus signs and any differences of zero. Remember that 2 or more identical values are given a mean value. For example there is a 3 at rank 3, and another 3 at rank 4, so both 3's are give the mean between ranks 3 and 4, ie. 3.5. Similarly there are three values of 6 occupying ranks 8, 9 and 10, so the mean is 9.

Difference	Differences sorted	Rank	Rank order of differences	Sign of sorted differences
+8	-1	1	1	-
+5	-2	2	2	-
+6	-3	3	3.5	-
+4	+3	4	3.5	+
-1	+4	5	5	+
+3	-5	6	6.5	-
+6	+5	7	6.5	+
-2	-6	8	9	-
-6	+6	9	9	+
-3	+6	10	9	+
0	Ignore			
-5	+8	11	11	+

There is no need to match the decimal places in these tables.

The next step is to add all the positive differences, called R^+.

$R^+ = 3.5 + 5 + 6.5 + 9 + 9 + 11 = 44.$

Now add the negative differences, R^-.

$R^- = 1 + 2 + 3.5 + 6.5 + 9 = 22.$

Finally we look up the critical value for R for the number of non-zero differences on the table. Although we have 12 trees, one of the differences is 0 and so we have only 11 functional values. Part of the table is given below. The full table is on page 55.

Number of non-zero differences	5% Level of significance
11	11
12	14
13	17

For 11 non-zero differences the critical value is 11. If the smallest of our two values for R is equal to or less than the critical value for R we reject the null hypothesis. Our smallest value is 22 and so we accept the null hypothesis - *There is no difference between the area of moss coverage on the north and south sides of the trees.*

.

Summary

- The critical value is found by using the number of non zero differences.
- Compare the smallest value of R with the critical value.
- If the smallest value of R is greater than the critical value then there is no significant difference between the two sets of data.
- The null hypothesis H_0 can be accepted.
- If the smallest value of R is equal to or less than the critical value then there is a significant difference between the two sets of data.
- The alternative hypothesis H_1 can be accepted.

Testing for an Association

❖ Chi-squared test.

This test is the one to use if the data –
- Is at the categorical level,
- Each measurement is independent from the others,
- The expected frequencies are greater than 5.

You should not use the test if any of the expected frequencies fall below 5.
The formula is -

$$\chi^2 = \sum \frac{(O-E)^2}{E}$$

Where
O = the observed result, and
E = the expected result.

The expected result may be based on the null hypothesis as can be seen in the second example below. In a genetics question though you can predict the frequency of the offspring on the expected Mendelian ratio, eg. 3:1 or a 9:3:3:1 ratio.

One-column and Two-column Tables

There are two types of table you are likely to come across, the one-column table and the two-column table. This simply refers to the number of columns of observed results. Which ever it is always set out your data and calculations in a table.

Calculating a χ^2 for a One-column Table

The number of columns is always 6, and the number of classes of data determines the number of rows.

Example 1. A student collected the seeds from an F_1 hybrid of tall and short varieties of a new form of rockery plant. She then grew the seeds, expecting a ratio of 3 tall to 1 short plant. She obtained 400 offspring altogether.

Variety	Observed O	Expected E	O - E	$(O-E)^2$	$\frac{(O-E)^2}{E}$
Tall plants	285	300	-15	225	0.75
Short plants	115	100	+15	225	2.25
Totals*	*400*	*400*	*0*		$\Sigma = 3.0$

* The totals row is not really necessary, but it helps prevent calculation errors. The totals of the Observed and Expected columns must be the same, and the total of the O - E column must = zero.

So we have a chi-squared value of 3.0. Before looking this up on the table we need to determine the number of degrees of freedom. This is simply the number of classes minus 1. Here we have 2 classes – tall plants and short plants, so the number of degrees of freedom = 2 – 1 = 1.

The χ^2 values for one degree of freedom are given below. The full table is on page 56.

	Significance level				
df	50%	10%	**5%**	1%	0.1%
1	0.46	2.71	3.84	6.63	10.83
	Not significant		Significant - fairly confident	Highly significant - very confident	Very highly significant almost certain

We now look on the table along the row for 1 degree of freedom and find where our number, 3.0, lies. In this case it is between 2.71 and 3.84. Our significance value is therefore between 10% and 5%. In biology we use the 5% value as the changeover point. Less than 5% means significant; greater than 5% means not significant. Now remember what the test is doing – comparing the expected and observed result. The significance is whether the difference between expected and observed is significant or not. If it is significant then something happened specifically to cause the difference; if it is not significant then the actual difference seen is simply due to chance, maybe too small a sample size. Our result of 3.0 means that the difference between the expected ratio of 3:1 and the observed ratio of 2.48:1 is not significant at the 5% level, or to put it another way, this result is likely to occur between 5 and 10 times in 100.

Example 2.

Crabs are able to prize limpets off rocks, and a marine biologist wanted to see if the size of the limpet determined if it was attacked by the crab. She selected male crabs all with the same shell size and placed 10 in each of three tanks that had been stocked with 50 of each of two different sized limpets. She recorded the number of limpets attacked during a 24-hour period.
Her null hypothesis was – '*The size of the limpet has no effect on whether it is attacked by the crabs*'.

	Number of limpets eaten in 24 hours	
Tank number	Small size	Large size
1	42	23
2	36	30
3	40	27
Total	*118*	*80*

Variety	O	E	O - E	$(O-E)^2$	$\frac{(O-E)^2}{E}$
Small size	118	99	19	361	3.65
Large size	80	99	-19	381	3.65
Totals	*198*	*198*	*0*		**Σ = 7.3**

Again we have 1 degree of freedom, and this time our value of 7.3 falls between 1% and 0.1%. This means the difference is highly significant because the probability of it occurring by chance is between 1 and 0.1 times in 100, and thus the null hypothesis is rejected. In other words, the crabs did prefer the smaller limpets.

Calculating a χ^2 for a Two-Column Table

Here we have two sets of observations as before but this time there are two categories so all together there are four sets of observations. Before setting out our standard table as above we need to set out an initial table called a 2 x 2 contingency table because it has two rows and two columns.

Example

The marine biologist also wanted to know if two different species of limpet occupied different heights above low water. She collected random samples of the limpets near the low water and the high water mark and counted the number of each species.

Region	Number of limpet species 1	Number of limpet species 2	Region totals
Upper shore	24	18	42
Lower shore	15	31	46
Species totals	39	49	Grand total 88

Her null hypothesis was

'There is no difference in the numbers of the two species from the upper and lower shores'.

To calculate the expected numbers for a species in a region we multiply the total number of the species by the total number found in the region and divide by the grand total.

Region	Number of limpet species 1		Number of limpet species 2	
	O	E	O	E
Upper shore	24	$\frac{39 \times 42}{88}$ = 18.6	18	$\frac{49 \times 42}{88}$ = 23.4
Lower shore	15	$\frac{39 \times 46}{88}$ = 20.4	31	$\frac{49 \times 46}{88}$ =25.6

Degrees of freedom is (number of rows – 1) x (number of columns -1) = (2 – 1) x (2 – 1) = 1 x 1 = 1.
For 1 degree of freedom the critical value is 3.84.

We can now set out our standard chi-squared table.

Limpet species	O	E	O - E	$(O-E)^2$	$\frac{(O-E)^2}{E}$
1 upper shore	24	18.6	5.4	29.16	1.57
1 lower shore	15	20.4	-5.4	29.16	1.43
2 upper shore	18	23.4	-5.4	29.16	1.25
2 lower shore	31	25.6	5.4	29.16	1.34
Totals	*88*	*88*	*0*		**Σ = 5.59**

The chi-squared value of 5.59 is greater than the 5% critical value of 3.84. This means that there is a significant difference between the observed and expected values for the distribution of the limpets. Thus species 1 does prefer the upper shore and species 2 the lower shore and the null hypothesis has been disproved.

Summary

- Degrees of freedom = number of classes - 1
- 5% is the significance level or a probability of 0.05.
- If the calculated value is less than the critical value then there is no significant difference between the sets of data.
- The null hypothesis H_0 can be accepted.
- If the calculated value is greater than the critical value then there is a significant difference between the sets of data.
- The alternative hypothesis H_1 can be accepted.

❖ The Spearman Rank Correlation

This test is the one to use if the data –

- Is at the ordinal or interval level;
- Has between 7 and 30 values.

For convenience, the measure of correlation lies between +1 for a perfect positive correlation, and –1 for a perfect negative correlation. The formula for the Spearman Rank correlation, r_s, is –

$$r_s = 1 - \frac{6\sum D^2}{n(n^2 - 1)}$$

D is the difference between the ranks, and n is the number of pairs of values.

Example

When walking her dog through a woodland a student noticed that the number of plants at ground level varied, and so did the intensity of light reaching the ground due to different species of tree. She went back later and collected the following data.

Site	Light intensity / lux	% cover by plants
1	300	86
2	600	46
3	500	39
4	100	15
5	100	41
6	400	52
7	900	100
8	800	63
9	200	60
10	500	30
11	700	72
12	1100	71

Table 1. Data collected from 12 woodland sites of light intensity and % plant cover using a 50cm quadrat.

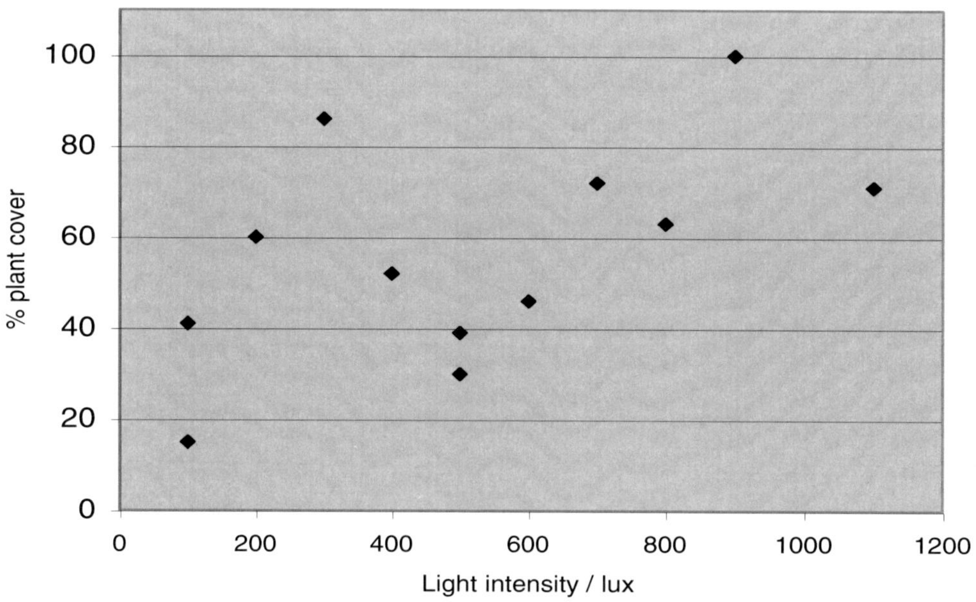

Graph 1. Scattergraph of light intensity against % plant cover.

Her null hypothesis was – *There is no relationship between the light intensity and % plant cover.*
She thought there was a slight positive correlation with these sets of data, but to be sure she carried out an analysis using the Spearman Rank correlation, r_s.

The first step is to rank the data for each variable. You can sort data in a simple Word table.

Light intensity / lux, sorted	Rank
100	1.5
100	1.5
200	3
300	4
400	5
500	6.5
500	6.5
600	8
700	9
800	10
900	11
1100	12

There is no need to match the decimal places in these tables.

% cover by plants, sorted	Rank
15	1
30	2
39	3
41	4
46	5
52	6
60	7
63	8
71	9
72	10
86	11
100	12

Now calculate the difference D and then D^2.

Site	Light intensity / lux	Rank R_1	% cover by plants	Rank R_2	$D = R_1 - R_2$	D^2
1	300	4	86	11	-7	49
2	600	8	46	5	3	9
3	500	6.5	39	3	3.5	12.25
4	100	1.5	15	1	0.5	0.25
5	100	1.5	41	4	-2.5	6.25
6	400	5	52	6	-1	1
7	900	11	100	12	-1	1
8	800	10	63	8	2	4
9	200	3	60	7	-4	16
10	500	6.5	30	2	4.5	20.25
11	700	9	72	10	-1	1
12	1100	12	71	9	3	9
				Sum	0	129

$$r_s = 1 - \frac{6\sum D^2}{n(n^2-1)}$$

$$r_s = 1 - \frac{6 \times 129}{12 \times 143}$$

$$= 1 - 0.45$$

$$r_s = +0.55$$

Number of pairs of measurements	Critical value
9	0.68
10	0.65
12	0.59
14	0.54

<u>Table of critical values.</u>

We now compare our value with the critical value on the above table. (The full table for 30 pairs of measurements is on page 56). We have 12 pairs and the critical value is 0.59. Our calculated value of r_s = 0.55, which is less than the critical value, and so there is no correlation between light intensity and % plant cover. Thus the null hypothesis is supported. Note though that 0.55 is very close to 0.59 so that her original thought that there appeared to be a slight positive correlation was not far wrong. (0.55 is a positive number hence showing a positive correlation).

Summary

- The critical value is found by using the number of pairs of measurements.
- If the calculated value is greater than the critical value then there is a positive correlation.
- If the calculated value is less than the critical value then there is a negative correlation.
- The greater the calculated value is from the critical value the greater the gradient.

Section 1.4.2

Statistical Formulae and Tables

Variance

$$s^2 = \frac{\sum (x-\bar{x})^2}{n-1} \quad \text{or} \quad s = \frac{n\sum x^2 - (\sum x)^2}{n-1}$$

Standard Deviation

$$s = \sqrt{\frac{\sum (x-\bar{x})^2}{n-1}} \quad \text{or} \quad s = \sqrt{\frac{n\sum x^2 - (\sum x)^2}{n-1}}.$$

If you are using Excel the formula used varies depending on the version of Excel.

Critical Values for the t-test and Related t-test.

t-test, unequal variances.

$$t = \frac{|\bar{x}_1 - \bar{x}_2|}{\sqrt{\frac{s_1^2}{n_1} + \frac{s_2^2}{n_2}}}$$

Where $\bar{x}$ = mean, s^2 = variance, and n = number in sample. 1 and 2 are samples 1 and 2.

Related t-test

$$t = \frac{\bar{d}}{\sqrt{\frac{\sum d^2 - (\sum d)^2 / n}{n(n-1)}}}$$

Where $\bar{d}$ = the mean of the differences between the pairs of values, and n = the number of values in the sample.

Degrees of freedom	Significance level Probability				
	20% 0.2	10% 0.1	**5% 0.05**	2% 0.02	1% 0.01
14	1.34	1.76	**2.14**	2.62	2.98
15	1.34	1.75	**2.13**	2.60	2.95
16	1.33	1.75	**2.12**	2.58	2.92
17	1.33	1.74	**2.11**	2.57	2.90
18	1.33	1.73	**2.10**	2.55	2.88
19	1.32	1.73	**2.09**	2.54	2.86
20	1.32	1.73	**2.09**	2.53	2.85
21	1.32	1.72	**2.08**	2.52	2.83
22	1.32	1.72	**2.07**	2.51	2.82
23	1.31	1.71	**2.07**	2.50	2.81
24	1.31	1.71	**2.06**	2.49	2.80
25	1.31	1.71	**2.06**	2.49	2.79
26	1.31	1.71	**2.06**	2.48	2.78
27	1.31	1.70	**2.05**	2.47	2.77
28	1.31	1.70	**2.05**	2.47	2.76
29	1.31	1.70	**2.04**	2.46	2.76
30	1.31	1.70	**2.04**	2.46	2.75
40	1.30	1.68	**2.02**	2.42	2.70
50	1.30	1.67	**2.00**	2.40	2.67
60	1.29	1.67	**2.00**	2.39	2.66
120	1.28	1.65	**1.98**	2.15	2.61
	←	decreasing	significance	increasing	→

Degrees of freedom = (sample 1 + sample 2) - 2

Note that at the bottom of the table the degrees of freedom jumps by 10 but the significance values change only by a small amount. It is therefore not worth including all the intermediate values.

Critical Values for the Mann-Whitney U test

You should have a minimum of 7 values for each set. If you have 15 or more then check to see if you could have used the t-test – the data will have to have a normal or near normal distribution.

n1	5	6	7	8	9	10	11	12	13	14	15
n2											
5	2	3	5	6	7	8	9	11	12	13	14
6	3	5	6	8	10	11	13	14	16	17	19
7	5	6	8	10	12	14	16	18	20	22	24
8	6	8	10	13	15	17	19	22	24	26	29
9	7	10	12	15	17	20	23	26	28	31	34
10	8	11	14	17	20	23	26	29	33	36	39
11	9	13	16	19	23	26	30	33	37	40	44
12	11	14	18	22	26	29	33	37	41	45	49
13	12	16	20	24	28	33	37	41	45	50	54
14	13	17	22	26	31	36	40	45	50	55	59
15	14	19	24	29	34	39	44	49	54	59	64

$$U_1 = n_1 \times n_2 + \tfrac{1}{2} n_1 (n_1 + 1) - \Sigma R_1$$

$$U_2 = n_1 \times n_2 + \tfrac{1}{2} n_2 (n_2 + 1) - \Sigma R_2$$

Where -
n_1 is the number of samples in set 1;
n_2 is the number of samples in set 2;
ΣR_1 is the sum of the ranks in set 1;
ΣR_2 is the sum of the ranks in set 2.

Critical Values for the Wilcoxon Matched Pairs test

	Significance Level Probability			
N_D	20% 0.2	**5% 0.05**	2% 0.02	1% 0.01
5	0	**--**	--	--
6	2	**0**	--	--
7	3	**2**	0	--
8	5	**3**	1	0
9	8	**5**	3	1
10	10	**8**	5	3
11	13	**11**	7	5
12	17	**14**	9	7
13	21	**17**	12	9
14	25	**21**	15	12
15	30	**25**	19	15
16	35	**29**	23	19
17	41	**34**	27	23
18	47	**40**	32	27
19	53	**46**	37	32
20	60	**52**	43	37
21	67	**58**	49	42
22	75	**65**	55	48
23	83	**73**	62	54
24	91	**81**	69	61
25	100	**89**	76	68
26	110	**98**	84	75
27	119	**107**	92	83
28	130	**116**	101	91
29	140	**126**	110	100
30	151	**137**	120	109
	← decreasing	significance	increasing →	

Critical Values for the Chi Squared Distribution

$$\chi^2 = \sum \frac{(O-E)^2}{E}$$

Where
O = the observed value, and
E = the expected value.

	Significance Level Probability				
Degrees of freedom	20% 0.2	10% 0.1	**5% 0.05**	2% 0.02	1% 0.01
1	1.64	2.71	**3.84**	5.41	6.64
2	3.22	4.61	**5.99**	7.82	9.21
3	4.64	6.25	**7.82**	9.84	11.34
4	5.99	7.78	**9.49**	11.67	13.28
5	7.29	9.24	**11.07**	13.39	15.09
6	8.56	10.65	**12.59**	15.03	16.81
7	9.80	12.02	**14.07**	16.62	18.48
8	11.03	13.36	**15.51**	18.17	20.09
9	12.24	14.68	**16.92**	19.68	21.67
10	13.44	15.99	**18.31**	21.16	23.21
11	14.63	17.28	**19.68**	22.62	24.73
12	15.81	18.55	**21.03**	24.05	26.22
13	16.99	19.81	**22.36**	25.47	27.69
14	18.15	21.06	**23.69**	26.87	29.14
15	19.31	22.31	**24.00**	28.26	30.58
16	20.47	23.54	**26.30**	29.63	32.00
17	21.62	24.77	**27.59**	30.00	33.41
18	22.76	25.99	**28.87**	32.35	34.81
19	23.90	27.20	**30.14**	33.69	36.19
20	25.04	28.41	**31.41**	35.02	37.57
	←	decreasing	significance	increasing	→

Degrees of freedom = Number of classes - 1

Critical Values for the Spearman Rank Correlation.

Number of pairs of measurements	Critical value
5	1.00
6	0.89
7	0.79
8	0.74
9	0.68
10	0.65
12	0.59
14	0.54
16	0.51
18	0.48
20	0.45
22	0.43
24	0.41
26	0.39
28	0.38
30	0.36

$$r_s = 1 - \frac{6\sum D^2}{n(n^2-1)}$$

Where
D = the difference between the ranks, and
n = the number of pairs of values.

Section 1.5

Creating shortcuts when using Microsoft Word

cm^3

Typing cm^3 is tedious since you are likely to do it a lot and you have to use it since it is the SI unit.
Set up an autocorrect.
Type cm3 and format it to cm^3.
Highlight all of it and then go to File and click Options.
Click Proofing and then click Autocorrect Options near the top.
cm3 will already be in the with box.
Type c3 in the Replace box and select the Formatted text circle. The cm3 in the with box now changes to cm^3.
Click Add.
Click OK and OK.

Now all you need to do in order to type say $25cm^3$ is to type 25c3 and AutoCorrect will change it to $25cm^3$.

^0C

Again use AutoCorrect.
Type 0c (This is a zero not a capital O).
Format it to ^0C.
Highlight all of it and then go to File and click Options.
Click Proofing and then click Autocorrect Options near the top.
0C will already be in the with box.
Type .0c in the Replace box (include the full stop) and select the Formatted text circle. The 0C in the with box now changes to ^0C.
Click Add.
Click OK and OK.

Now all you need to do in order to type say 25^0C is to type 25.0c and AutoCorrect will change it to ^0C. The full stop is necessary because AutoCorrect would not recognise say 200c as 20^0C. It may seem a little slower to have to put in the full stop but it is certainly quicker than using the mouse to highlight the 0 and then superscripting it.

±

This is available from Insert – Symbol but it is tedious to keep having to do this. A quicker way is to create a shortcut on your keyboard. I use Alt= simply because the + symbol is on that key which makes it easier to remember and it is not used by anything else.
Go to Insert - Symbol.
Click More Symbols.
Choose the Font you are using.
From the drop-down subset box select Latin-1 Supplement.
Select the ± symbol.
Select the Shortcut Key box hold down the Alt key and type =. Alt+ = appears in the Press new short cut key box.
Click Assign.
Click Close and Close.
Now all you need do to insert a ± is hold down the Alt key and press =.

Standard Error and Confidence Intervals

This is taking the statistics in your analysis in a slightly different direction and this could be valuable in the Analysis part of your Extended Essay.

Standard deviation is a measure of the variation about the mean. However your mean is just the mean of your sample from the complete 'population', so it is called the <u>sample mean</u>, and is only an estimate of the <u>true mean</u> of the population. If your sample size is small, your estimate of the true mean won't be as good as an estimate based on a larger sample size. Look at the two graphs below.

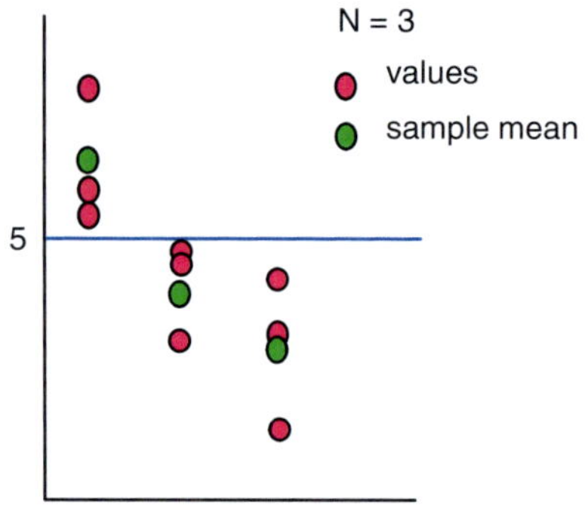

I have taken 3 samples of 3 from a population which has a true mean of 5. The first sample happened to be three observations that were all greater than 5, so the sample mean is too high. The second two samples have three observations that were less than 5, so the sample means are too low.

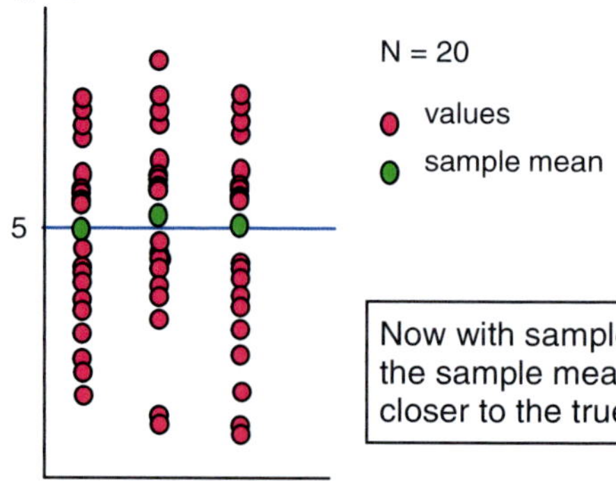

Now with samples of 20 the sample mean is much closer to the true mean.

You may want to indicate how close your sample mean is likely to be to the true mean and this can be done using standard error of the mean. If you take many random samples from a population, calculate the mean for each one, then the standard error of the mean, SE_M,* is the estimated standard deviation of these different sample means.

* Always say standard error <u>of the mean</u> as there are standard errors for other statistical measurements.

Calculating standard error of the mean is easy –

SE_M = standard deviation* ÷ √ sample size

*See page 19.

It is obvious that the larger the sample size the smaller the standard error.
If your graph is plotting the mean values as the dependent variable then your uncertainty bar can be standard error of the mean rather than standard deviation.

You will recall that for normal distributions about 68% of the values would be within plus or minus one standard deviation of the mean, and about 95% would be within plus or minus two standard deviations. Exactly the same percentages apply to standard error of the mean, ie, about 68% of the sample means would be within plus or minus one standard error of the true mean, and about 95% would be within plus or minus two standard errors of the true mean.

Confidence Intervals

We can use this information to determine confidence intervals, ie how confident can we be that our sample mean is close to the true mean.
In Biology we most commonly use the 95% confidence interval. This means that if altogether you took 100 samples and calculated the confidence limits for each sample, then 95, ie 95%, of those samples would contain the true mean within the confidence limits and 5, ie 5%, would not.
(You will recall from the t-test, chi squared and Wilcoxon tests we always took the significance level at 5%).
You are very unlikely to be taking 100 samples, so you are counting on the fact that the one that you did is not one of the 5.

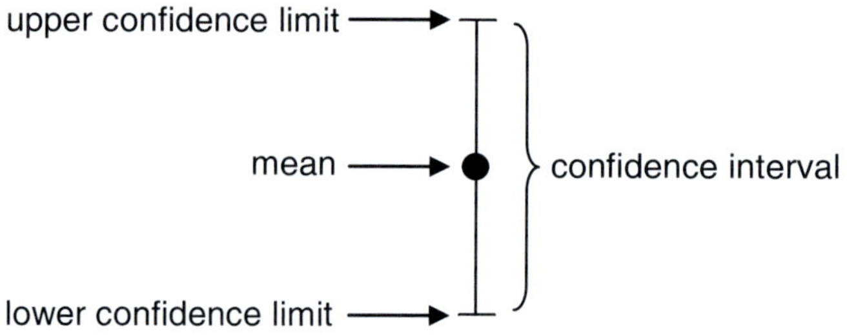

To calculate the confidence limits we use the formula below.

95% confidence limits are - **mean ± t x standard error of the mean**

How do we find the value of t? This depends on our sample size, n and is given in the table below.

n	5	6	7	8	9	10	11	12	13	14	15	20	25	30	40	>40
t	2.78	2.57	2.45	2.37	2.31	2.26	2.23	2.20	2.18	2.16	2.15	2.09	2.06	2.04	2.02	2.00

Example
A sample of 16 peas had a mean mass of 10.0g with a standard deviation of 2.0g.

$SE_M = 2 \div \sqrt{16} = 0.5g$

The 95% confidence limits for the mean would be –

10 ± (t x 0.5)   From the table above t = 2.15 for a sample size of 16.

10 ± (2.15 x 0.5) = 10 ± 1.08g

This means that you can be 95% confident that the true mean lies between 8.92 to 11.08g, the confidence limits for this particular sample.

One and Two-tailed Tests

If we are able to make a prediction of the result of an investigation, as in examples 1 and 2 below, then we need to look at the 'confidence' of our prediction, ie how confident are we that the change in the independent variable <u>will</u> cause a specific change in the dependent variable, or <u>might</u> cause a specific change in the dependent variable. (It does not matter which direction the change is.)
If we are very confident then we use a one-tailed test, but if we are not sure then we would use the two-tailed test.
The examples below are the same ones as on page 41.

Example 1. A new selective weedkiller is being tried out on a field. Half the field is sprayed with the weedkiller and the other half sprayed with water as the control. We could put forward both types of hypothesis.
The null hypothesis states that *'There is no difference in the weed population in the two halves of the field after treatment'.*
The alternative hypothesis states that *'The weedkiller decreases the number of weeds in the half of the field where it is used'.*

Example 2. Ivy growing in the shade will have less light available for photosynthesis whereas one growing on a sunny wall will have plenty of light. The leaves are likely to be different in size.
The null hypothesis would state that *'There is no difference in the surface area of the leaves of the shaded plant and leaves of the sunny plant'.*
The alternative hypothesis states that *'The surface area of the leaves of the shaded plant is greater than the surface area of the leaves of the sunny plant".*

The significance test then confirms which hypothesis to accept and which to reject. If the null hypothesis is accepted then there is no difference between the samples; if rejected then there is and we may be able to accept the alternative hypothesis.

Example 3. A student investigated colour vision in bees by putting sugar water in glass dishes above different coloured paper to see if they preferred yellow to blue. Here we have no idea which colour the bees would choose – it would be pure guesswork and so we cannot state an alternative hypothesis.
The null hypothesis states that '*Bees have no preference for yellow or blue*'.
If we then prove the null hypothesis to be wrong we know that the bees do prefer one colour over the other and the numbers will tell us which is the preferred colour.

In example 1 we could assume that the new weedkiller is effective because it would have already undergone lab testing and so we can use the one-tailed test because we are predicting only one result – the weedkiller is more effective.

In example 2 we have good scientific reasoning that the leaves in the shade will have a larger surface area so that they can collect more light for photosynthesis and so again we can use the one-tailed test because we are predicting only one possible results – the surface area is greater.
However with the one-tailed test we must remember that if a significant result is obtained it is only acceptable if it is in the predicted direction. In example 2 for instance we may find that there is a significant difference but it is the sunny leaves that are bigger and not the shaded leaves and so we have to reject H_1. It could be that the shaded leaves are smaller but have more chlorophyll.
On the other hand for a two-tailed test all we need is a significant difference and either direction is acceptable.
Finally in example 3 we have to use the two-tailed test.

So why don't we always use a two-tailed test? In most cases in fact we would do, but it is more difficult to obtain a significant result, ie. there needs to be a greater difference between the means for it to show. Using the one-tailed test is therefore more sensitive and so if we can use it then the result will be more precise.

Look at the example on pages 42/43 and decide if you would use the one- or two-tailed test. The answer is on page 44.
Note that the probability value returned for a one-tailed test using Excel is exactly half the probability for the two-tailed test. Try it out using the data in table 3 on page 43. If we had used the one-tailed test we would obtain a probability of 0.001.

The Problem Graph

Here is the graph again. (I've made it much smaller to save space.)

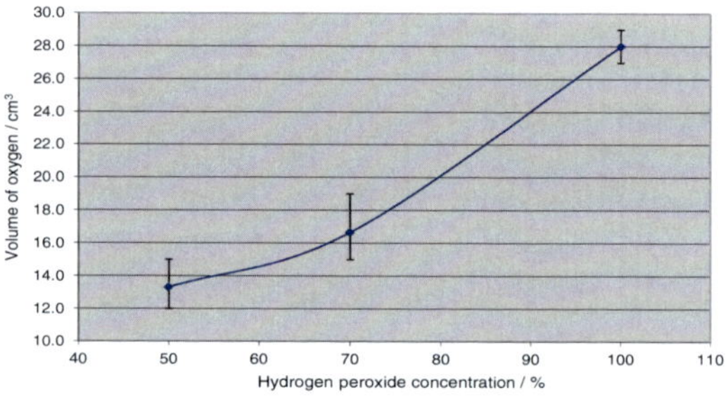

What volume of oxygen would you predict should be released if the hydrogen peroxide concentration was zero, ie the control with water? It should be zero, but if you extrapolate the line backwards it looks as though it is going to level off at around $12 cm^3$.

Here is the graph again but with both the hydrogen peroxide concentration and the mean volume of oxygen at zero.

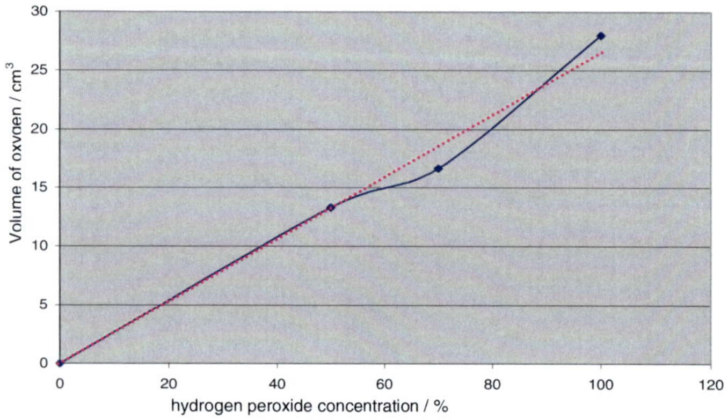

It would be reasonable to expect the relationship to be linear but we cannot draw a straight line through the points.

However, now let's add the uncertainty bars.

I can now draw a straight line making use of the uncertainty bars.

Clearly my original design was faulty because I did not include the control and this would have led me to make incorrect conclusions.

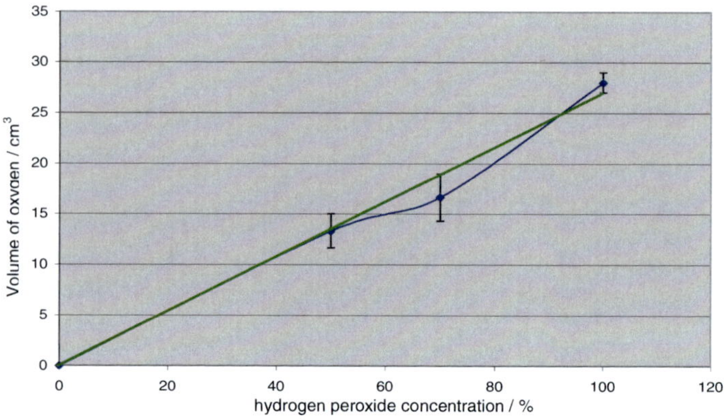

Sinus Blocknose
1.1.13

A Practical Write-up Headings Template

Name and date in Header

In italics under each heading are hints and reminders.

Design

Research Question
What is the effect of X (independent variable) on Y (dependent variable)?

Background Information
Biological knowledge.
Maybe include a hypothesis.

Variables

Independent	*Include the range.*
Dependent	*This is **exactly** what you will be measuring.*
Controlled	*List all of them.*
Uncontrolled	*Think – maybe they can be controlled.*

Apparatus
List.
Use SI units.
Be precise.

Risk Assessment
State risk and method of reducing.

Method
Describe in detail exactly and precisely how you carry out each step – timings, measurements, equipment.
Make it clear how the controlled variables are kept constant.
Have you included a control?
Keep each step in the correct sequence.
Use separate paragraphs – even bulleted/numbered list.

Data Collection and Processing

Results and Analysis
Tabulate results.
Include units and uncertainty in column headings.
Make use of the uncertainty bars on graphs.
Tables and graphs with clear and precise titles.

Statistical Formulae
Formula and method of calculation.

Conclusion and Evaluation

Conclusion
Clear and precise statement or statements).

Explanation of Conclusion
Detailed biological explanation.
Refer to background information and hypothesis if stated
Refer to cited published data if available.
Do the results support the hypothesis?
Reference sources used.

Evaluation of Results
Look at range and frequency of independent variable.
Look at quality of data - standard deviation, accuracy, reliability, anomalies.
Look at line of best fit on graph with respect to plotted points and uncertainty bars.
Are there alternative lines?

Evaluation of Method
Comment on weaknesses in design and use of apparatus.
Comment on significance of those weaknesses with respect to reliability and accuracy of the data.
For each weakness suggest a significant improvement – simply collecting more data is not significant.
Keep these together, ie weakness 1 + improvement 1 ; weakness 2 + improvement 2 etc.
Aim for at least three improvements.

Page number in footer

Appendix - Plotting Uncertainty Bars with Excel 2003 (Excel calls them error bars).

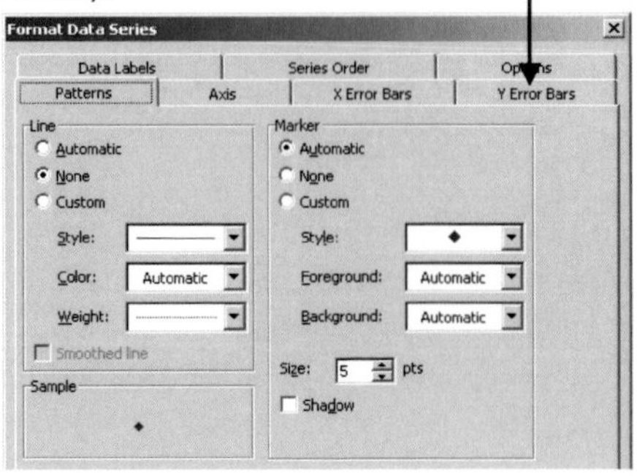

1. Uncertainty bars with the same value

Right click on one of the data points;
Left click Format data series;
Select Y error bars;
On the 'Display' bar select Both;
Select Fixed value and then use the arrows or type in the value you want.
Click OK.
Repeat for X error bars if required.

2. Plotting maximum and minimum

You would normally do this if you only have 2 to 4 values for each data point.

Suppose you are investigating the effect of concentration of hydrogen peroxide on the release of oxygen by catalase and you have collected the data in the following table in your Word document. Note for simplicity I have included only three values for the independent variable – in a real investigation you should have at least six.

Note use of the word Mean and not Average.

Hydrogen peroxide concentration / %	Volume of oxygen collected / cm^3			
	Set 1	Set 2	Set 3	Mean
50	13	12	15	
70	16	15	19	
100	27	29	28	

Try doing these examples for practice.

Copy and paste these on to your embedded Excel spreadsheet. Remember that this is not going to be visible so just include simple brief headings.
Calculate the mean – in the first cell below Mean, E2, type **=average(B2:D2)** ; **Enter**
Copy this formula to the other two cells and format the number to one decimal place.
Now transfer these calculated values to your Word table.
Select all the mean values, right click and Copy, go back to your Word table and go to the top cell, right click and choose Paste cells. This will paste each mean into the correct cell.
Your table should now be as below.

Hydrogen peroxide concentration / %	Volume of oxygen collected / cm^3			
	Set 1	Set 2	Set 3	Mean
50	13	12	15	13.3
70	16	15	19	16.7
100	27	29	28	28.0

1. Go back to your spreadsheet. Select your three values for the hydrogen peroxide, hold down the ctrl key and select the three values for the mean. Click on the Chart Wizard and select your graph – XY (Scatter) with points.
2. Excel automatically puts in a legend (the small box on the right which says Series1) which you won't want if you have just one dependent variable. Remove it in step 3. Sometimes though you will when you have 2 or more dependent variables. If you included the column heading when you were selecting the data then the legend shows which line is which dependent variable.
3. Do not add labels for the X and Y axes or the title here but add them later underneath it using Word text boxes. You can add or delete gridlines as required.
   Remove the Legend if you don't want it by selecting Legend and unchecking the box Show legend.
4. The final step. Check the box As new sheet. This places just the graph beneath your Word data table and not the Excel data table. This data though is still there on sheet 1 using the tabs at the bottom of the Excel window. If you change any of the data for any reason then the graph is automatically updated.

Go back to your Excel data table which is sheet 1 on the tabs at the bottom of the window..
Now calculate the difference between the mean and the maximum and minimum for each set of values.
Go to cell F2 and type **=max(B2:D2)-E2 ; Enter**. Copy the formula to the remaining cells.
Go to cell G2 and type **= E2-min(B2:D2) ; Enter**. Copy the formula to the remaining cells.

You should now have the data as below.

HP conc	Set 1	Set 2	Set 3	Mean	Difference between mean and maximum	Difference between mean and minimum
50	13	12	15	13.3	1.7	1.3
70	16	15	19	16.7	2.3	1.7
100	27	29	28	28.0	1.0	1.0

1. Go back to chart 1.
2. Right click on any of the points;
3. Select Format data series;
4. Select Y error bars;
5. Select Custom; The cursor should be blinking in the + box.
6. Left click on the small coloured box on the right end of the + box;
7. A window appears - Format data series – Custom +;
8. Return to your data on sheet 1 – the tabs are on the bottom of the display box;
9. The Format data series – Custom + is still there;
10. Left click and drag over the data column Difference between mean and maximum. In our example this is F3 to F5;
11. As you drag the cell references appear in the Format data series – Custom + box;
12. Now go to the Format data series – Custom + box and left click the small box on the right with the red spot;
13. The large window with Format data series reappears;
14. Move the cursor to the Custom – box and repeat steps 6 to 13 but this time selecting G3 to G5.
15. Left click OK;
16. The graph reappears with the maximum / minimum bars added;

If the bars do not have the small horizontal lines at top and bottom go to the chart, right click on any bar, select Format Error Bars and Patterns and select the horizontal line option. Your graph should look like the one on page 29.

3. Uncertainty bars with different values

Look back at the data and graph on page 16. You may have decided that as the volume of gas increased so did the uncertainty, giving you the following data table.

temperature / ^{0}C	volume of gas collected / cm^3
5	26 ± 1
10	39 ± 2
15	46 ± 3
20	51 ± 4
25	57 ± 5

- On the Excel table you will need to put the uncertainly values in a separate column.

By following the procedure described below for adding uncertainty bars you would then obtain the graph shown on page 28. You would then add the line either by hand or using the curved line drawing tool in Word.

If you have 5 or more values for each data point then you may be able to calculate standard deviation.

Suppose you are investigating the effect of concentration of hydrogen peroxide on the release of oxygen by catalase and you have collected the data in the following table. This is the same as on page 25 for Sets 1-3 but I have now added Sets 4 and 5. For simplicity I have kept to only three values for the independent variable – in a real investigation you should have at least six.

Hydrogen peroxide concentration / %	Volume of oxygen collected / cm^3						
	Set 1	Set 2	Set 3	Set 4	Set 5	Mean	Standard deviation
50	13	12	15	14	11		
70	16	15	19	15	17		
100	27	29	28	27	25		

Copy and paste these on to your embedded Excel spreadsheet as below. Remember that this is not going to be visible so there is no need to include all the detailed headings, though it is helpful to keep track of which column is which by putting in basic headings.

HP conc	Set 1	Set 2	Set 3	Set 4	Set 5	Mean	St Dev
50	13	12	15	14	11		
70	16	15	19	15	17		
100	27	29	28	27	25		

Calculate the mean – in the first cell below Mean, G2, type **=average(B2:F2)** ; **Enter**.
Copy this formula to the other two cells and format the number to one decimal place.
Now calculate the standard deviation. Type **=STDEV(B2:F2)** ; **Enter**.
Copy this formula to the other two cells and format the number to one decimal place.

HP conc	Set 1	Set 2	Set 3	Set 4	Set 5	Mean	St Dev
50	13	12	15	14	11	13.0	1.6
70	16	15	19	15	17	16.4	1.7
100	27	29	28	27	25	27.2	1.5

Now transfer these calculated values to your Word table.
Select all the mean values, right click and Copy, go back to your Word table and go to the top cell, right click and choose Paste cells. This will paste each mean into the correct cell.
Repeat for standard deviation.
Your Word table should now be as below.

Hydrogen peroxide concentration / %	Volume of oxygen collected / cm^3						
	Set 1	Set 2	Set 3	Set 4	Set 5	Mean	Standard deviation
50	13	12	15	14	11	13.0	1.6
70	16	15	19	15	17	16.4	1.7
100	27	29	28	27	25	27.2	1.5

Go back to your spreadsheet. Select your three values for the hydrogen peroxide, hold down the ctrl key and select the three values for the mean. Click on the Chart Wizard and select your graph – XY (Scatter) with points and continue through the steps. See page 56.
Remember to save your graph as a new sheet.

1. Go back to chart 1. The tabs are at the bottom of the window.
2. Right click on any of the points;
3. Select Format data series;
4. Select Y error bars;

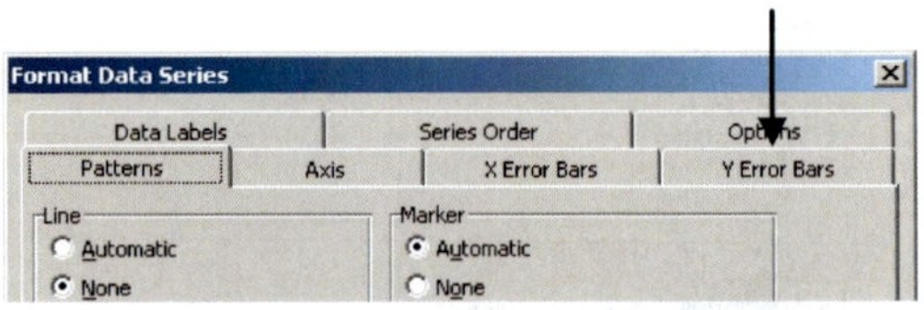

Select Custom; the cursor should be blinking in the + box.

5. Left click on the small coloured box on the right end of the + box;

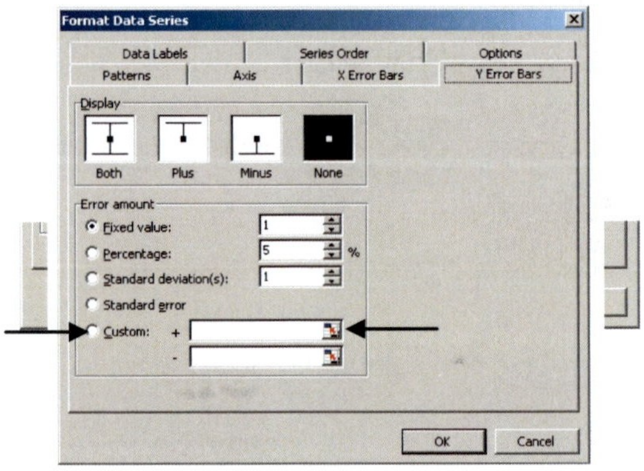

6. A window appears - Format data series – Custom +;
7. Return to your data on sheet1 – the tabs are on the bottom of the display box;
8. The Format data series – Custom + is still there;
9. Left click and drag over the data column Standard deviation. In our example this is H3 to H5;
10. As you drag the cell references appear in the Format data series – Custom + box;
11. Left click on the small box at the right end and the Format data series box reappears.
12. Move the cursor to the Custom – box and again drag the mouse over the data on sheet1. The references appear in the box.
13. Left click OK;
14. The graph reappears with the standard deviation bars added.

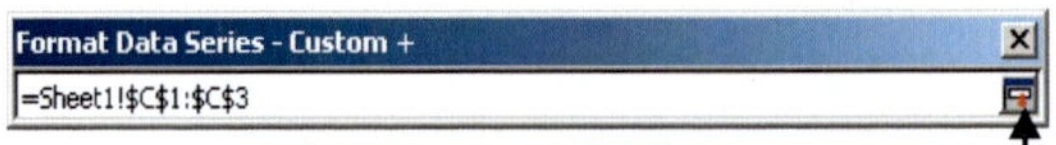

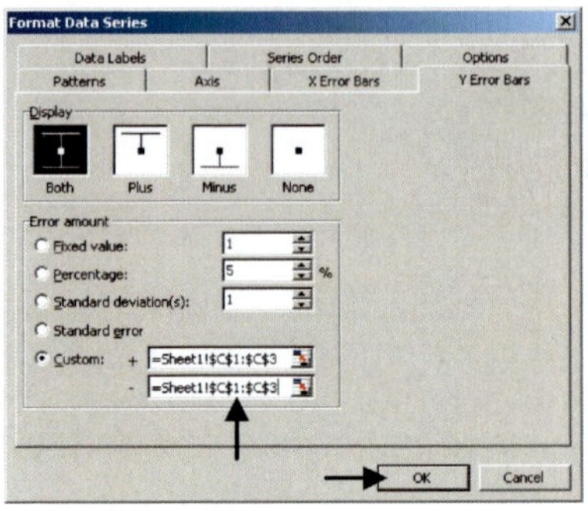

If the bars do not have the small horizontal lines at top and bottom go to the chart, right click on any bar, select Format error bar and select the horizontal line option. Your graph should look like the one on page 29.